MY GOD, MY MONEY

Finding Balance between Your Money and Your Faith

Judith Allwood

This book is not meant to give financial or legal advice. Please consult with professionals in these fields for advice.

ISBN: 978-0-615-34487-4

Cover design by Tracean Miller

Interior design by Amy Cole, a.c. studio l.l.c.

Edited by Linda Robinson and Carolyn Madison

Printed in the United States of America.

Revised 2013

For additional copies, contact:
judith@mygodmymoney.com
347-204-3673

Contents

Acknowledgments 1
Preface 3
Introduction 5
Where Does My Wealth Come From? 9
Truly Secure 13
The Source Of Wealth 17
A Gift From God 21
The Cost Of Wealth 25
Welcome To The Kingdom! 29
And Why Do You Worry? 33
My Neighbor's Things 37
Fair Day's Work, Fair Day's Pay 41
Aren't You More Valuable? 45
Satisfaction Guaranteed 49
What Is This Money For? 53
Help My Unbelief 57
What Will We Do Tomorrow? 61
Gratitude 65
Incentives For Letting Go 69
What Is More Important? 73
What's In Your Heart? 77
The Real Payday 81
Hope Thou In God 85
As A Man Thinketh 89

Wealth With Wisdom 93
The Habit Of Gratitude 97
Riches Without Godly Wisdom 101
Did You Ask? 105
Creative Survival 109
The Poor Among Us 113
Job Satisfaction 117
No Poverty Here 121
Relating To Money 125
How Should I Give? 129
The Best Part 133
Giving—It's A State Of The Heart 137
Free To Give 141
To Tithe Or Not To Tithe 145
Let God Be True And Every Man A Liar 149
A Growth Fund 153
For Generations To Come 157
The Cost Of Ignorance 161
What Shall We Eat? 165
These Final Words 169
Why Worry? 175
Index 177
Notes 183

To my dad, who first recognized my writing aptitude,
to the memory of my loving mom,
to my stepmom,
and to all of my siblings
with love.

Acknowledgments

The idea of this book was inspired by the circumstances of my personal life, those of my family and friends, and the Christian community at large. Its production has been the direct or indirect result of contributions from some very special people: my former pastor, Dr. Russell McLeod, who first impressed upon me the necessity of journalizing one's personal devotional insights; Deverton Gilphilin, who has consistently fanned the flames of my passion for writing; Diane Butturff, whose contribution to my path in relating to money is priceless.

I also am extremely grateful for Sylvia Gilfillian, who constantly was my sounding board and had a healthy appetite for the book; Elthia Wilson, my sister and friend, who identified with, shared, or challenged some of my childhood escapades; my beloved sister Gloria Pemberton, who believed in me and who, in her true big-sister style, held me to account every step of the way; and Margaret Tucker, my charming little sister, for endlessly dreaming of my publishing success.

I also thank Janice George-White for holding me accountable; Joanna Major for her optimism and support; Margaret Gordon-Rowe for her loving contribution; Donna Duncan-Scott for her love and generosity and for enrolling me in believing in myself; Diana Morgan-

Burgess for her inspiration; Junie White for her long-lasting friendship; and Teddy Crawford for always encouraging me to keep writing.

I extend appreciation to all of my other siblings, nieces, and nephews for their love and encouragement. I am especially grateful for all of my readers as you diligently take this journey with me. Linda Robinson, my content editor—you are a rare gift of genius and insight. I truly admire your tremendous talent.

Above all, I thank God Almighty who loves me more than I can ever comprehend, whose servant I am, who instructs me and guides me in the best pathway for my life, who counsels and watches over every intricate detail of my life. For in you and through you and by you are all things, today and forever. Thank you.

Preface

In my early years, I learned that "it is easier for a camel to go through the eye of a needle than for a rich man to enter the kingdom of God" (Luke 18:25). Afraid of risking the eternal promise, I renounced riches, resulting in the formation of beliefs and attitudes that kept me in ongoing financial despair. Tired of subsistent living, I embarked on an inquiry into what God has to say about money, wealth, and riches. What are they for? Should I desire them? How should I handle them? The effort has evolved into this book, unfolding four primary purposes for money.

Money does have the power to ensnare the person who is ignorant of its true functions. It can deceive the mind into thinking that it can offer true security. But those who are spiritually enlightened use it for:

- Worshipping God
- Expanding his kingdom
- Personal sufficiency and enjoyment
- Blessing and enriching others

Affirming God as our source inspires our dependence on the One who gives us the ability to create wealth. Trusting in his enduring providence frees us from greed, hoarding, stinginess, inequity, fear, anxiety, scarcity, and worry—so that we may become faithful stewards of what he has entrusted to us.

Introduction

For most of my adult years, I tried hard to "have money." My efforts at overtime hours, better-paying jobs, gigs on the side, get-rich-quick attempts, investment strategies—even the lottery—had all been what King Solomon calls chasing after the wind.[1] Somehow I never seemed to be able to get my hands on what people call "some good money." I had often wondered why. Was it that money always eluded me, or was it that *I* found money elusive? I had been reflecting on this for a while when I came across some ideas in a little book that encouraged me to examine my opinions and beliefs about money, wealth, and riches. I soon started to see how my confusion may have kept me incapable of realizing financial goals beyond a certain level. Maybe it was *I* who had found money elusive after all!

I started to take a close look at the way I thought and spoke about money, and found that words I would use to describe rich people had included *rotten* and *filthy*. My concept of wealth had been "the rewards of exploitation," and the very thing for which I longed I dubbed *a necessary evil*. I began to evaluate my reasons for wanting money, the meanings I attached to having or lacking money, and what I tended to do with it whenever I would get it. I found that my attitude toward money had been anything but positive.

Because I had been taught that "it is easier for a camel to go through the eye of a needle than for a rich man to enter the kingdom of God,"[2] I had made concerted efforts to not contemplate ever having a lot of this supposed evil that served only to separate people from God. My utmost desire is to please God, and I wanted to be sure that I was not offending him. In fact, the thought of ever becoming rich made me feel so ungodly and uncomfortable that I tried to not entertain it. Besides, simply speaking the words brought on an overwhelming sense of embarrassment and shame. I remember needing to get a book from the library, and because it had the word *rich* in the title, I struggled to tell the librarian the name of it.

While I had made attempts to increase my earnings, the objective was never to have much more than I would need to pay my bills. All I asked for was just a little extra for a rainy day. Invariably, I would get more bills, and the rainy days were sure to come—often demanding more than I had set aside, and I would grudgingly part with my little savings. This pattern of persistent lack and financial insufficiency made me question why I and many other children of the God who owns the earth and everything in it were so often broke and needy.

As the real world offers no substitute for this "dreaded evil," I found it necessary to search out what God has to say about the matter. Within that context, I found balance and harmony, addressed my beliefs about it, and became clear about its place in the life of the believer in God. The astounding findings have had me unlearn some pseudo-Christian ideologies and cultural myths. I continue to be enlightened regarding its true value and its workings in manifesting God's glory, utmost purpose, and immense goodness. Thus I am learning to relate to money in a wholesome and guiltless fashion. The experience has been liberating, enlightening, and simply rich.

I invite you to explore with me, over the next forty days, some of what God has said in his Word about money, wealth, prosperity, and riches. My hope is that you will give yourself the freedom to think about your own beliefs regarding the subject, and that you would be open to being transformed and enriched in your spiritual walk.

I encourage you not to rush through, but to read only one lesson each day and allow room to reflect on new thoughts and discoveries that may arise. I have listed questions at the end of each section with spaces for you to write down your own thoughts, feelings, and persuasions.

This is not intended to be a theological report. It is a devotional format that came out of my personal journey. Some of the scriptural references may challenge your own views and interpretations, so I encourage you to just take a look at what is possible; be open to the Spirit's leading, and as Paul instructed, "Be persuaded in your own mind."[3] Use the prayers at the end of each thought to guide your own dialog with God. Please also feel free to write to me at judith@mygodmymoney.com. May you be enlightened and built up in your faith.

Where Does My Wealth Come From?

The Lord sends poverty and wealth, he humbles and he exalts.

—*1 Samuel 2:7*

As I meditate on this verse, I think of Job, who had enormous wealth. The Bible says, "He was the greatest man among all the people of the east."[4] Yet in one day, he lost everything he owned including all his ten children. If there was ever anyone who knew that one cannot serve God and money, it was Job! He was totally devoted to God and did not practice evil. When everything was taken from him, being totally conscious that it was God who had given him all his possessions anyway, he acknowledged that God in his sovereignty had chosen to take them away.

Personal disasters can occur in the life of anyone—the wealthy, the poor, and all others in between. And when they do, the attitude with which we respond speaks loudly about who we really are. Some people are able to respond to God's faithfulness and wisdom. Yet, others are not so inclined. They are more likely to curse God and die, as Job's wife advised him to do. These people cannot take the bitter with the sweet, as the saying goes. They cannot detach themselves from the things they own, so if they should lose those objects, their lives would become meaningless and not worth living.

What is your attitude when you meet defeat? Are you able to grasp that "the Lord gave and the Lord has taken away?"[5] Or are you more inclined to become upset and blame God for the things that he has removed or allowed to be removed from your life?

Let us look on the flip side of the scenario: What would you do if you became significantly wealthy? Would you applaud yourself for having possessed the skills and wit to acquire riches, or would you count it as a gift from God for which he is due maximum credit? What is your most prized possession? How does it serve you? Is it in any way a testimony of God's faithfulness, or do you use it simply to satisfy *your* purposes?

I believe that the way a person handles money is a test of both moral and spiritual character. We are spiritual beings for whom the function of wealth is no different from the function of poverty as far as maturity in Christ goes.

A friend of mine expressed anxiety that her husband's success could become an obstacle to his faithfulness and humility to God. I shared with her a saying that I had heard in passing: "More money only makes you more of what you already are." So I don't think the money creates characteristics in people. I believe it brings out what is at the core of who you are.

Acknowledging God's sovereignty is a big struggle for both those who walk with him and those who do not. The way I see it, it is not so much the material things that God is interested in blessing us with, for we will be separated from those things at some point. What God intends is to build character in us that will outlast everything else. That, I believe, exemplifies true wealth.

> *Father, sometimes I forget who really is in charge, yet you have made everything to be subject to you. I am in awe of you because you have created all things! I submit to you as you continue to build my spiritual character. I open my arms and heart to receive from you. Amen.*

Reflection on Where Does My Wealth Come From?

What is your current personal economic status?

What do you see as the purpose of it?

How is it improving or affecting your relationship with God?

What specific lessons are you learning?

Truly Secure

Though your riches increase, do not set your heart on them.

—Psalm 62:10b

A woman shared her success story at a financial forum. Only five years prior to that day, she was unemployed and living on government subsidy. She had no savings and was unable to find a job for which she was qualified. Hearing about the possibility of investing in real estate, even with no deposit, she decided to give it a try. In a few short years, she had gone from being nearly homeless to being the owner of a number of homes. Her income increased significantly. It could happen to anyone willing to do the work. Your riches can increase. You can become a millionaire.

But why do you think anyone would want to set his or her heart on riches? When I once called a friend with whom I hadn't spoken for a long time, he asked in jest, "What happened? You got rich and switched?" This is not unusual behavior in people who have had monetary increase. Attitudes do change; people have been known to turn from families, friends, and God as they become financially strong. However, there is a difference between external riches and true wealth. It is the external kind that affects a person's behavior in this way.

What will your attitude be when your wealth increases? (Or would you rather opt for "just enough" so that you will not have to deal with any such likelihood? Give it some thought.) The psalmist, in his wisdom, and maybe from experience, admonishes, "Do not set your heart on it,"[6] for it is fleeting. It takes only one misfortune to wipe it all away. It is unwise to get comfortable with increased riches so much that your relationship with God and people gets compromised. If anything can make you lose sight of God, trusting in money and acquisitions will. The deceptiveness of money can cause you to disregard right morals and spiritual soundness.

Setting your heart on your increase can also cause you to get locked into less than what God wants to make available to you. You could miss many wonderful opportunities in the time and effort you take to clutch what you have so tightly. As we have learned, God is the source of our wealth. It seems wiser, then, to become fully aligned with the Creator of wealth instead of with the wealth itself. In this way, we can hear his instructions and respond to him in obedience.

Not only can fixating on riches blur your vision, it also has the ability to harm you psychologically as you isolate yourself from others. Many people find themselves in this predicament out of fear that sharing their possessions will deplete what they have amassed. Their sense of worth is confused with their net worth, so they fear that they will lose personal value by being separated from their money. But the truth is that a person's real worth cannot be measured monetarily in spite of what society teaches.

If you want to be truly wealthy, focus your attention on building spiritual character so that if you become financially successful, it will not become a snare to you.

When all is said and done, it is not the amount that you were able to acquire but how you were able to manage and administer your acquisitions that God will reward. Remembering that wealth comes from the Lord ought to make you conscious of the fact that he has the power to send poverty as well. So, although your riches increase, do not get wrapped up in it.

Giver of all things, I commit all aspects of my life to you. Thank you for giving me opportunities to make money and increase my net worth. Let me never get confused about the focus of my worship and adoration. I put nothing before you, not even my money. Amen.

Reflection on
Truly Secure

Recall a time when you received a certain sum of money. Did you notice any difference in the way you felt?

What feelings did you notice?

What bearing did it have on your sense of security?

How do you equate your personal sense of worth with your financial worth?

Take stock of your possessions. What is it that you possess in the greatest quantity? What does this say about what you have been pursuing with your life?

The Source Of Wealth

It is he who gives you the ability to produce wealth.
—Deuteronomy 8:18a

One of the things that prompted me to write this book was my desire to explore why there is such a prevalence of poverty and lack among God's people, I having been one of them. The Word does say that the Lord sends poverty, but I believe it is more as a life lesson than a lifestyle. So why do some of us live that way perpetually? Is it that we believe there is virtue in poverty? Is it that our expectation of God is limited? Is it that we think and speak more in ways that support destitution than in ways that support affluence

In today's text, we read that God gives us the ability to produce wealth. So what hinders us? In the past, I have felt almost sacrilegious to think, read, speak, or study about money or riches or even the possibility of having wealth. But apart from the guilt, I also held the belief that I did not have what it would take for me to experience abundance, so I limited myself to just earning a living, only enough.

Because I viewed rich people as being cruel, stingy, unapproachable, crooks, exploiters of the poor, unworthy of the kingdom of God, and a host of other negative things, I could not see myself becoming one. I eventually came to find out that not all rich people have these characteristics. In fact, if you think about it, most of the things that we benefit from in our world are the results of the efforts of the rich. Many of them acquired their assets through their honest pursuits of education, dreams, visions, hard work, and perseverance, and have used their God-given abilities to produce wealth.

This is not to say that some people have not acquired wealth by very dishonest, immoral, and ungodly means. Theirs will not last, and God will surely punish them! The Bible says, "Better a poor man whose walk is blameless than a rich man whose ways are perverse."[7]

A very good friend of mine told me that he has to be realistic and work at a regular job (even though he hates it and it doesn't utilize his natural abilities and talents), then go after his passion when he has made enough money. He reminds me of the Matthew 25 servant who said that he was afraid, so he dug a hole in the ground and there hid the resources that his master had entrusted to him.[8] Believing in your abilities is not just a hot topic for a motivational seminar; it is the way to make the most of yourself. God designed us with talents according to our abilities, and we are responsible for developing and utilizing them. The same fear that influenced the servant also grips many of us who hide beneath the illusion of "job security." If you desire a lifestyle that will allow you to enjoy more, do more and give more, you can start by dismantling your belief that you can't, or that wealth is not for the child of God. He gives you the ability to produce wealth of every kind, not just financial wealth.

I believe there would be more harmony and peace in this world if there were more fulfilled workers exposing their God-given talents. Sometimes getting there calls for us to literally stop what we are doing as a job (the way an aircraft does just before it takes off soaring into the sky) and take the steps to launch into God's intention for our individual calling. He gives you and me the ability to produce, and I believe that financial wealth is one way in which he rewards us for honoring what he has equipped us with. He is pleased when we use the resources that he has given us to serve him and humanity. I want to hear him say to me, "Well done, good and faithful servant!"[9] How about you?

Dear Lord, how unwise and miserable it is to use tools that you did not give. Teach me not to despise, but to honor the gifts that you have invested in me to create spiritual, social, and financial wealth. I will trust and obey you, for only then will I find true fulfillment in my work. Give me the courage to walk by faith. Let your will for my life be done on earth as it is in heaven, for Christ's sake. Amen.

Reflection on
The Source of Wealth

What do you think about having riches and abundance?

What are your abilities, talents, and skills?

How are you developing and using those abilities right now?

Do you believe that *your* abilities can help you to produce substantial income? If yes, how, and where can you start?

A Gift From God

I will also give you wealth, riches and honor,
such as no king who was before you ever had.
—2 Chronicles 1:12b

It is not an uncommon perception that the wealthy are wicked, dishonest, and immoral people who get their riches from evil schemes, and so are categorically denounced and abhorred. Chief among critics are those who have very negative ideologies about money. Yet look at God's promise to Solomon: "I will give you wealth." If we knew the wealthy Solomon not as a Bible character, is it probable that we would regard him with scorn?

If God provides an abundance of money and possessions to his people, where does our negative perception and contempt of it come from? Could it be a façade that some of us wear to appear pious and humble? Or could it be because Jesus has said to the poor, "Blessed are you," and to the rich, "Woe to you?"[10] (See Luke 6:22 and 24.)

Let us take a look at the context within which Jesus spoke these words. He challenged the proud attitudes and dishonorable motives of those whose values rested only on material things. Their initiatives often got them enormous wealth, and they believed that their riches were the ultimate goal or achievement in life. Jesus observed that it was woeful that their quest for fulfillment was only through earthly riches, which can neither last into eternity nor truly satisfy. It is to this shallowness that he spoke. He did not denounce riches simply for the nature of it (because money itself is neither good nor bad), but for what the seekers of it made it mean.

The poverty that Jesus taught about (in the beatitudes of Matthew 5) was of the spiritual sort. Material poverty itself is not a virtue that makes a person fit for the kingdom. Those who acknowledge their state of spiritual hunger and poverty, and seek after righteousness will be satisfied. When we make right and faithful living our priorities, God gives us wisdom in all things—including the pursuit of the purposes for which he created us.

God told Solomon to ask for anything he wanted, and Solomon asked for wisdom and knowledge to lead God's people. God was pleased with where Solomon's heart was, and he added the gifts of wealth, riches, and honor. Solomon's intention was not to accumulate wealth on earth, but to please and take care of what mattered to God, i.e., his people. In simple terms, Solomon's request sounded like this: "God, give me wisdom and knowledge to do the best job of leading those over whom you have put me in charge, for my judgment is poor, and it affects my way of doing things. But if you teach me, I will know what to do, and you will be pleased—for that is the only thing that I desire." God gave Solomon the tools to do the job effectively.

His faithfulness continues through all generations. Therefore, when we commit ourselves to his service, he may choose to equip us in wealth, riches, and honor;

however, we must remember their purposes and never allow them to entangle us.

> *Lord, I have seen men and women on whom you have bestowed monetary gifts get deceived by the thing you gave them to perform your works. I do not count myself to be above reproach, and it is only you who can keep me faithful. Fill my hunger and thirst for righteousness, I pray. Amen.*

Reflection on
A Gift From God

What purpose have you used your money to serve?

How do you describe or respond to people who are rich by honest means?

What are some things that you use or enjoy on a regular basis?

Do you see any of these as the efforts or contributions of the wealthy?

The Cost Of Wealth

Do not wear yourself out to get rich; have the wisdom to show restraint.
—Proverbs 23:4

Take a moment to imagine what a worn-out person might look like: persistently tired, jaded, and lethargic, maybe. Yet those are only reflections of the physical and mental realms. In this state of fatigue, a person cannot reasonably expect to be inspired.

The story is told of a young entrepreneur whose ambition was to become a multimillionaire by the age of forty. In his late twenties, he had already reached millionaire status. He made his wife and children materially comfortable, but they were not happy, for they rarely saw each other. While he was out cutting more deals, his wife was home suffering from loneliness. She decided to file for divorce. That awareness prompted the young man to refocus his commitment to his family and God, and taking Jesus' instruction to the rich young ruler of his day, this man sold all his possessions and gave the proceeds to people in poverty.

This story has a happy ending for the man whose fear of the Lord impressed him to not lean on his own understanding but acknowledge and submit to God's ability to direct his paths. I wish this was the case for more of us who are so anxious about success, fame, and materialism. We would probably spend a great deal less in medical expenses and would not ail from depression and other mental and physical conditions. We are not all called to "sell all of our possessions and give to the poor," but as people of God, we have to cultivate the willingness to do so if he requests that we do. We are not mandated in the scriptures to seek riches, but we are instructed to seek godly wisdom and to govern each and every aspect of our lives.

I really do not believe that a person makes a wise decision in choosing to make money his or her goal. There is a popular saying that goes like this: do what you love and the money will come. Develop the gifts and talents that God has given you. Pursue your calling and purpose, and you will find fulfillment and financial reward. The person who makes money his ambition might do just about anything to achieve it. He runs the risk of wearing himself out.

Are you able to enjoy the things that you work multiple jobs to pay for? What is your pursuit of money costing you? When you're done working, do you still have the energy to play with your baby or listen to your teenager? What about your talents and abilities? Are you able to share them with your church family or the general community? Is your hard work bringing you more quantity or more quality? How much more do you really need to enjoy the fruits of your labor?

The millionaire we just read about came to see what really matters—love for humanity, not acquisitions. Obsession with riches wears you out. Money is not all you need. You die and leave it anyway, or like Proverbs 23:5 says, "It sprouts wings and flies away."

If you find that you do not have the will to resist chasing money, ask God to intervene. Look for ways to invest in others by expressing love, kindness, goodness, generosity, and material blessings. Store up treasures of the heavenly kind; this is the wealth that will last forever. This is the wealth worth pursuing.

Lord, please help me to understand what true wealth is and to put emphasis on what means the most to you—humankind. How easy it is, Lord, to lose sight of my truest calling, which is to love others. Accept my willingness to do your will and please you, I pray. Amen.

Reflection on
The Cost of Wealth

How many hours do you spend working each week?

How many hours do you sleep? Exercise?

How much time do you spend in quiet meditation, reflection, and prayer?

What difference do you think spending more time with your family does or will make?

Some people think that increased income will make their family happier. What do you think?

Welcome To The Kingdom!

It is easier for a camel to go through the eye of a needle than for a rich man to enter the kingdom of God.

—Mark 10:25

I was just a little girl when I first heard this scripture verse in church. The priest had put it in terms that we could relate to by having us imagine someone trying to insert the thickest rope into the eye of a regular sewing needle. Learning that this effort was virtually impossible, I retained the mental picture to remind me to never risk my chance of entering heaven by ever acquiring too much money.

It wasn't until I started this study that I realized that I didn't really know what *rich* implied. By then I had started to learn about relating to money. I was watching a video of a seminar in which the presenter interacted with a member of the audience on this said scripture reference.

"How much money would it take to make you rich?" he asked the participant.

"I don't know," the gentleman responded contemplatively. In that moment, I became aware that the gentleman's response was exactly what my response would be if I were asked the same question. I had spent years protecting myself from something about which I knew absolutely nothing. I had been living from a script that I had interpreted to mean, "If you want to make it into heaven you must resent money." Is it any wonder that I was always so broke and in need?

It became clear when I read the text and discovered that Jesus *did not say* it was impossible for a rich person to enter heaven (neither did the priest, by the way). What he said was that it is *hard* for a rich man to enter the kingdom of God (italics mine). See Matthew 19:23. As I read, "With God all things are possible," I began to find even more freedom from the fear of becoming rich. Anyone who places trust in God is welcomed into heaven, rich and poor alike.

You might agree with me that money—no matter what the currency—is one of the supreme powers known to humanity. It makes possible medical research, technological advancement, attainment of personal goals such as education, and buying of anything that can be bought—including freedom from slavery. Despite these facts, however, we should remember that God is supreme and he rules over all, including money.

Job, Solomon, and other faithful, rich patriarchs knew and placed God first in their lives. Their vast wealth did not obstruct their faith in God. It did not obstruct their reverence for him or their obedience to his commandment: "I am the Lord, your God ... You shall have no other gods before me. You shall not make an idol ... worship them or serve them."[11]

God accepts everyone in spite of his or her status in

life. He welcomes into his kingdom those who acknowledge him and are humble enough to admit that they are powerless to redeem themselves.

Dear Lord, there are times when my trust in the power of money vies for my faith in you. Help me to always remember where its power stops. There is no end to your power through which there is peace, joy, true happiness, and, most of all, eternal life. I thank you that nothing can separate me from your love. Amen.

Reflection on
Welcome to the Kingdom

What are your personal views on this verse?

Are you afraid of what opening up yourself to God might lead to? For example, he could ask you to give up everything. Are you intimidated by that possibility?

How might you resolve that fear?

Do you think the love of God is keeping you from the deceptiveness of wealth?

And Why Do You Worry?

Do not worry about tomorrow, for tomorrow will worry about itself.
—Matthew 6:34

It was a sweltering summer day when haze shimmered above the surface of paved roads. Driving to work, I rolled the car windows down to let some cool air in. As hot air filled the car, I drove on expecting cool breezes to start flowing with my increasing speed. Suddenly, I became aware of my thought process: I was refusing to turn on the air-conditioning because I wanted to save the gas for a future time. Simply put, I worried that what I had would run out, and I would have to spend my money, which I would rather hold on to a little longer.

How foolish! I thought as I turned on the air conditioning and meditated on what it means to tell myself, "I cannot afford it." What a freeing encounter that turned out to be!

Jesus shared a parable of a rich man who, like me, saw fit to store things up for the future.[12] Speaking of the fact that the future is not promised to anyone, God rebuked him for being a fool, asking him who, upon his passing, would inherit what he had chosen to hoard. I, too, felt rebuked as I reflected on my habit of stockpiling and being stingy. While it is not unwise to save and conserve, proper boundaries must be constructed to separate healthy habits of saving from practices of miserliness. It is a thin line! The mentality of scarcity is like any other malady that keeps one from living a healthy life, a life of true faith, trust, and belief in Providence.

God assures us that he will provide, and that we ought not to worry about life and its perishable things, for life is more important than food[13] or any other basic requirements (including gas to operate air-conditioning units in cars.) The ability to trust that the Father has been pleased to give us the kingdom requires much more than a little faith. We have to be as trusting as little children and accept the Word without judgment.

What about you? What are you caught up in worrying about? What keeps you awake at night? Do you believe that your Father knows that you need those things? Can you, by worrying, add a single hour to your life? If life is more important than food, then we do not need food to sustain the kind of life to which Jesus referred. It is faith that we need and it is impossible to please God without it.

God tells us to busy ourselves with learning about him and his kingdom. When we are fully assured of who he really is, we have no difficulty trusting him. Out of relating to God intimately, we find out what he wants from us; we get to understand that he did not make us for our purposes but for his. Our God is totally committed to enabling us to fulfill his purpose. When we get that, we become less concerned with the things that he has already said he would take care of. We can choose to seek his kingdom of righteousness (which comes by faith), peace (which he gives to those who focus on him), and joy (which we find abundantly in his presence). Or we can take on the affairs of everyday life, obsessing about the future so much that the blessings in the present moment escape us. Which do you choose?

> *Lord, whenever I get anxious about life's necessities, please remind me that your source never runs low. Help me to shift reliance on my resources to my faith in you, for the sake of your purpose. Amen.*

Reflection on
And Why Do You Worry?

Are you often carried away in thought about the future?

What is the nature of the things you get anxious about?

What can you do to change these things?

My Neighbor's Things

You shall not covet your neighbor's house ... or anything that belongs to your neighbor.
—Exodus 20:17

Covet: *to inordinately or culpably desire what belongs to another.* Covetousness is one of the sins that easily beset us. We do not always set out to covet. In fact, sometimes we are not even conscious that we are being selfish in our desires. We see others getting along and deep in our hearts, we wonder why the favor did not come to us instead. Someone is jubilant, and we don't share fully in her joy because we feel denied in some way. This behavior can arise out of the deep-rooted belief that there is not enough to go around—an untruth that has the power to enslave the mind and breed fear and greed.

One of the most common grudges that we tend to hold has to do with money, wealth, riches, or their products. Countries wage wars out of envy and individuals kill others because of it. The first recorded murder in Scripture resulted from envy.[14] (See Genesis 4:8.) Still, some of us badmouth, put down, or condemn the "snobbish wealthy" or "the filthy rich" out of covetousness.

Maybe you aren't quick to admit it, but if you take a look deep into your soul, you may find even the slightest bit of resentment toward someone you perceive as being more successful than you. That could include a complete stranger driving a better-looking car than yours. Have you ever noticed that?

What are some of your desires? What is your *deepest* desire? How do you feel when an acquaintance achieves an objective similar to yours? Do you brim with excitement for her, or do you brood? Maybe you just respond with indifference? Yes, envy can be that subtle. One proven fact is that when we envy people for their better positions or possessions, we, by that same effort, drive those very things away from ourselves. It is no wonder God commanded, "Thou shall not covet."

Have you ever felt that the better jobs, suitors, and opportunities are all gone? Ever felt as though you are always a little too late? That is scarcity-thinking. Those thoughts that have been put into your subconscious by your experiences, teachers, parents, or politicians serve no other purpose than to debilitate, discourage, and disillusion. The good news is we can let go of those thoughts and choose to retrain our minds with the kinds of thoughts that uplift us!

Transformation occurs when we replace ideas that do not serve us well with those that do. Practice becoming aware of your thoughts and see if they are godly. Ask the Holy Spirit to search your soul and help you to meditate on whatever is true[15]—there is enough to go around. The Word says, "The streams of God are filled with water to provide the people with grain ... Your carts overflow with abundance."[16] Remember, belief comes about by thinking the same thing repeatedly. God instructs us to meditate on his Word day and night. He satisfies the desires of every living thing from his limitless resource. He cannot lie. Think on those things.

When you begin to believe this availability of supply and start to allow the stream of God to flow toward you, you will find that you are more inclined to love your neighbor as yourself rather than to covet anything that belongs to him or entertain thoughts that are evil.

Dear Lord, your Word is truth, and the truth brings freedom. Embed it deep within me that I might not sin against you. Teach me to be thankful for what I have and not be jealous of others' property. Help me to let go of fear that it will run out, or that I will end up a loser. Amen.

Reflection on My Neighbor's Things

What dreams are you still waiting to come true?

Let's say you found out that someone else achieved a similar dream. How would you feel toward him?

Spend some time thinking about those emotions and your underlying fears or beliefs. Ask God's intervention to remove those that do not serve His purpose.

Fair Day's Work, Fair Day's Pay

Don't hesitate to accept hospitality, because those who work deserve their pay.
—Luke 10:7 (NLT)

Although in this text, Jesus was instructing his disciples to be receptive to hospitality in the mission field, I believe it is fitting in regard to our receptiveness of generosity, wages, and compensation—even outside of the missionary arena.

A forum of alternative health care practitioners discussed the matter of setting charges for their services. Almost all of them revealed that they tended to charge their patients very small fees. Why? They collectively felt that because of the benevolent nature of the services they provided, it was not right or decent to ask for more. It had nothing to do with the patient's ability to come up with more, or even whether the quality of the service warranted it—which it undoubtedly did—but everything to do with what *they*, as individuals, thought they deserved.

Feeling undeserving is quite a common conditioning. Perhaps you have experienced it too but aren't aware of its effect on your emotional, spiritual, social, or financial well-being. How do you feel about what you charge for your services or goods or what you accept for a salary? If it is below the going rate, is it because you feel guilty or embarrassed, or is it because you are afraid to be viewed as greedy for money? Have you ever told yourself that you aren't worth more?

Jesus saw the need to counsel his disciples to not be hesitant to accept deserved compensation, and some of us need that same advice today. We are often our own worst critic. We engage in self-condemnation and deny ourselves goodness. This continues the accusations or criticisms of ourselves that someone else may have started during childhood. We fail to see our own virtues. Or we may be constantly judging and failing to forgive ourselves. Do you see how we can retard our own success, relapsing each time we come close to getting a breakthrough? To make matters worse, we may not even be conscious of it.

Maybe you feel that you aren't worth much. But like the psalmist (Ps. 139), you can observe that God's works are wonderful, and that could begin to help you change your perception of yourself. You are God's valuable creation "worth more than many sparrows."[17] True humility does not call for you to put yourself down but rather to appreciate what God has graciously invested in you and made available for and through you.

The feeling of unworthiness can also get in our way of accepting God's grace, mercy, and forgiveness, which he gives freely to all. Jesus encourages us to be accepting of kindness and well-earned compensation. Look into your soul and see where you are holding back from yourself, and start practicing the habit of receiving with gratitude. If Jesus says, "don't be hesitant to accept hospitality," what should hold you back? Notice the way you respond to favors and offers from friends and family. If you tend to decline their gestures, remember what Jesus said. Use the opportunity to evaluate your self-worth.

> *Lord, I thank you for this awareness. Please help me to start the healing process today, redeeming myself and accepting your redemption as well. Cause me to appreciate the wonder that I am. Teach me how to be open to receive from you, others, and myself. Amen.*

Reflection on
Fair Day's Work

What ideas, thoughts, or expressions about money, wealth, or riches can you remember hearing when you were growing up? (For example, "Money doesn't grow on trees," "Look after your money and it will look after you," and "Rich people are ungodly.")

What part do you think they play in your current handling of money?

Have you or has anyone ever told you that you are undeserving?

Take another look at today's text, meditate on it, and make it yours.

Aren't You More Valuable?

You are more valuable to God than a whole flock of sparrows. And you are far more valuable to him than any birds! And since we are his children, we are his heirs. In fact, together with Christ we are heirs of God's glory.
—Luke 12:7b, 24b; Romans 8:17 (NLT)

A young lady shared her excitement about her extra earnings for the week. As I listened to her glee, a surge of embarrassment covered me, for the sum she was so happy about approximated what I earned in only a fraction of that time. I quickly stopped myself from feeling uncomfortable by recognizing that where I was financially was only a result of certain choices I had made. And the same was true for her. Moreover, she was being appreciative and grateful for what she found to be a meaningful week's salary.

As I worked through what had made me feel so sad, I realized that I felt that I didn't have the right to have more than anyone else. Who was I to deserve better, higher, more? How dare I have more? Shame on me! Contemplating this for the next several hours made me see the reason for the lack of abundance in my experience, for if God had ever blessed me extraordinarily, I would probably have died of guilt. I felt ashamed for having good things in my life.

I was still very young when an adult member of my family told me that I didn't deserve to share something that my other siblings were enjoying. I began to believe that I wasn't good enough to have certain things. I have battled with that undeserving feeling all my life and have often made some really mediocre choices as a result. I have found reassurance in today's texts. I choose to affirm that there is no condemnation to those who are in Christ Jesus, for those who live and walk not after the dictates of the flesh but after the dictates of the Spirit. This has brought healing to me.

I wonder if you also believe that you do not deserve either the things you currently have or the things you aspire toward. Maybe you hold yourself back from certain advancements because of these limiting beliefs. Therein lies your fear of success. You dare not have that better-paying job, that nicer living accommodation, or that higher education. You may have been told you that you were not good enough, and like me, you have believed. But just as you believed what you were told then, you can choose to believe what you are told now. You are more valuable to God than any bird!

God's glory is about the highest and best that anyone could ever yearn for. And he has given us the privilege to be identified with him. Christ has made us accepted in the Beloved. How freeing! God, King of the Universe, accepts me, faults and all. And he continues to perfect me so as to present me faultless before the presence of the Almighty!

You can begin to replace those false beliefs by speaking the truth found in God's Word, by seeking counseling and coaching, and by ceasing to put yourself down. Print Bible verses and post them where you can see them. Say them aloud. Just say them now, and see the shift in the way you feel. Like God told Joshua, meditate on them day and night. You will eventually start believing and experiencing changes in your life. When the negative thoughts enter your mind, go back and speak them over and over until they take root.

Dear Lord, I thank you for making me your child. You have crowned me with glory and honor and have made me a little lower than the angels. You denounce every judgmental accusation against me. Thank you for the work that you have started in me. Thank you for accepting me. Amen.

Reflection on
Aren't You More Valuable?

Can you identify an aspect of your life in which you feel undeserving? If yes, what is it?

What would you need to do or be in order to feel worthy?

How do you feel about your current income level? Do you think you deserve it?

Do you feel that you hinder God's goodness toward you by imposing guilt upon yourself?

Satisfaction Guaranteed

I have learnt in those circumstances in which
I am, to be satisfied in myself.
—Philippians 4:11b (DARBY)

At first reading, I was not very encouraged by these words by Paul because I thought it meant that I should be content in my state of lack and not pursue a fuller life. But with maturity, I have come to realize the boundaries that those words set for us, especially in a society of so much consumerism, and in an age when so much is being so furiously and psychologically promoted to tease our emotions and sensibilities.

I believe that contentment is the state of being thankful. Discontentment, on the other hand, is dissatisfaction about what is missing from our lives. It is easy to focus on what is lacking, especially as advertisements and other marketing devices insist that more can be had, and that more is better. According to Howard Dayton "[The] advertising industry has devised powerful, sophisticated methods of persuading the consumer to buy. Frequently the message is intended to create discontentment with what we have." Submitting to this state of discontent can put us in a lot of financial woes. How easily we get caught in the net of "easy payments," which add to our mountain of indebtedness!

So if contentment is a way of *being*, then it is clear that it is not dependent on our having or not having—it is simply a choice that we make. And if we have little, we choose to be as content as we would be if we had plenty. How do we make this happen? By simply being grateful. There is always an opportunity to express gratitude, and by choosing to take stock of what we *do* have and not complain about what we *should* have, we find satisfaction.

The father of a disabled child lived with his family in a small apartment. Each evening as he returned home from a hard day's work, he would be greeted by foul smells and a pile of mess the child had created. He longed to be welcomed into a clean, spacious home with peace and quiet. Resisting the temptation to complain, he willed himself to give thanks that he had all that he needed for life each day.

Like the aged hymn implores, he counted his blessings one by one for what he had then and for what he believed he would receive. Instead of waiting until he realized his dream, he started giving thanks in his prevailing circumstances. That gave him peace of mind, which energized and motivated him to look for other ways to increase his income so that he could provide the comfortable home he visualized and trusted God to provide. Contentment is not necessarily automatic, but it can be practiced until it becomes perfect.

Are you feeling discontented in your present circumstances? Take a few minutes to write down five to ten things or people for which you are thankful. Do this once a day for the next seven days and watch your level of contentment rise. Each time you catch yourself grumbling or complaining, ask God to show you something in that situation about which you can express gratitude. Will yourself to see new opportunities or possibilities in those circumstances.

> *Lord, I truly thank you that I already have all that I need for life and godliness. Sometimes I overlook these as I delve into complaint and ingratitude. Please forgive me and help me to develop a new attitude to look for the beauty within the ashes and the rainbow in the clouds. Amen.*

Reflection on Satisfaction Guaranteed

What things do you tend to complain about most?

Describe the alternatives that you would prefer.

Would you describe yourself as being content? If no, how can you establish a state of contentment?

Does that require that your circumstances change first?

What if they never change?

What Is This Money For?

For the love of money is a root of all kinds of evil. Some people, eager for money, have wandered from the faith and pierced themselves with many griefs.

—1 Timothy 6:10

"Money is the root of all evil." I have heard this saying more times than I can recall, and many even say it is from the Bible. If money is the root of all evil, then shouldn't everything that it obtains be the fruits of evil? Look around you; observe with all your senses. How many things are you able to identify that came about without money, directly or indirectly? Do you notice anything evil about them? Money was required to produce the book you are reading. Are you getting the picture? The Bible says, "For the *love* of money is a root of all kinds of evil" (italics mine).

What is the *for* for? In the preceding verses, Paul cautioned the church about the motives of its financial and material pursuits. As it was then, it is imperative for us to understand the true role that money and material things serve, as well as the fundamental purpose for which God placed us here on earth. So how does a person *love* money?

Love in this context implies an acute emotional attachment to any object. Psychologists link this kind of attachment to the negative emotions of loneliness, fear, and insecurity. It tends to be focused on self-aggrandizement and the insatiable thirst for power. The lover of money is motivated by craving or greed, and her highest commitment is to make a profit at the expense of life and limb to satisfy selfish desires. It is the kind that leads to the destruction and misery to self and others, as in the case where a person desires the insurance benefits so badly that it drives her to murder a spouse or parent. She loses out, however, by getting a life or death sentence instead.

Jesus had his disciples reflect on the consequences of getting everything they want in this life and losing their eternal peace. Let's take this opportunity to contemplate that too. All kinds of evil do range from premeditated mass murders to petty white lies. The subtlety of evil moves the psalmist to ask God to search for any presence of it within him.[18] That is because sometimes our own consciences cannot be relied on for self-examination. A good litmus test, however, is to examine our ultimate motive to see whether our longing to preserve our own interests is creating a risk for others. Look to see whether you are relying on your own efforts or on God's, and whether you are being thankful to him. He is able to make us rich in every way,[19] and when we are clear about his purpose for money in our lives, we have no greed for it.

If your love of money has caused you to wander away from the faith and has displaced God in your life, you do not have to remain there. He welcomes your return. In fact, it is not his desire that any should perish. If you have caused harm to others in your efforts to rake in wealth, you can make restitution. You can ask for forgiveness. You can do that here and now, and begin to experience peace and freedom. You can learn to love God and his creation, and can come to see that money is just a thing to be used.

> *Father, I thank you that the truth sets me free from guilt and all other untruths that bind me. I embrace the reality that all good things, including riches, come from you. I give up greed and craving of every sort and embrace a lifestyle that is pleasing to you. Cause me to use my talents and gifts to establish your purpose for my life, that your will be done on earth as it is in heaven through Christ Jesus. Amen.*

Reflection on
What is This Money For?

What are you willing to risk to acquire money? Why?

How do you feel when you do not have money or do not have enough of it?

Help My Unbelief

Yet the LORD longs to be gracious
to you; therefore he will rise up to show
you compassion.
—Isaiah 30:18

It was four o'clock, and I had already awakened once before, even though I had gone to bed at only 12:15 that morning. The mind seems to do a great job of worrying and being anxious at that time of day. So when thoughts about unpaid bills and joblessness had come rushing in, I had consoled it by saying that God is my Shepherd and Provider who will meet all my needs. Why had the anxious thoughts returned, then? Did my mind fail to register the truth?

It became apparent to me that merely repeating Bible verses or religious phrases is never enough. Even coupling them with prayers is never sufficient if a person fails to bring consciousness to the power of God. That is why Jesus cautioned his disciples about using "vain repetitions."[20] Looking within, I found that I, too, was guilty of babbling. While I knew that the Bible verses were *true*, and that God *is* my Shepherd and Provider who *will* meet all my needs, the reality of the words did not seem as emphatic as the circumstances facing me at that time.

"Anything is possible if a person believes," Jesus answered the man who questioned his willingness to heal his son. "How long shall I put up with you [unbelieving generation]?" he chided.[21] That goes for this generation too. He yearns for us to embrace the fact that his grace is unconditional, and that there is virtually nothing that we can do to merit it.

We reject his offering when we doubt that what he says is really true and applicable to our personal conditions. So I had asserted that God is my Provider and I will never lack, but I did it only absent-mindedly. I had failed to connect with him and be unreservedly assured that our heavenly Father knows exactly what we need even before we ask. As a result, I missed out on the peace that would have kept my heart and mind and warded off insomnia.

We also fail to accept his gifts when we think that we have to be worthy before we can receive from God. God's grace does not take worthiness into account. Grace is God saying, "Here is this thing I have for you," be it of spirit or substance. Our part is simply to cast all doubt aside and take it with humility and gratitude. Neglecting to receive what God offers is not an act of reverence. It is denial of the goodness of the One who sends rain on the righteous and the unrighteous.[22] In order to receive, we must have faith.

To *have* means to hold in mind,[23] and *faith* is the assurance of things we cannot see. When we put it all together, we see that to have faith is to hold a mental picture of our request in the full assurance that we will receive it. This is a great challenge in the matter of believing, for it is so hard to focus on what we cannot see with our physical eyes. In this age of so many distractions, many of us have not learned, let alone mastered, the art of closing out the external world and focusing inwardly in spite of the happenings in the world.

This is an enormous task, and Jesus knew it when he said, "Apart from me you can do nothing."[24] He invites us and eagerly waits for us to know him to the point of relying on him. By accepting, we rise above the ordinary to walk on water, to mount up with wings like the eagle, to dream, to do anything—for nothing shall be impossible to them that believe.

Dear Lord, please help my unbelief. You are so gracious and merciful, yet the truth of it sometimes escapes me. Help me to indiscriminately accept your love, peace, joy, favor, and mercy. I want to be more aware of my thoughts and aspire to fill my mind with your truth no matter what. Please help me to do it, I ask. Amen.

Reflection on
Help My Unbelief

Reflect on the last time you were concerned about anything relating to finances. What was it like?

Do you feel that you have to meet certain criteria before you can receive favor from God? If yes, what criteria?

Are you able to accept that God's grace is available to you, and all you have to do is receive it?

What Will We Do Tomorrow?

Do not be anxious about anything, but in everything, by prayer and petition, with thanksgiving, present your requests to God.
—Philippians 4:6

One of humanity's biggest challenges is to really experience the present moment. We worry—never about the present, but about the future—such a misuse of our time, attention, and brain cells.

The imprudence of this habit is that we are not guaranteed the future about which we concern ourselves. So by worrying, we only pass up our opportunity to truly live right now. No matter how adverse or severe our circumstances, there is always hope. There is always something in the moment that is worth acknowledging and being grateful about.

A friend shared her anxiety about losing her home. I encouraged her to recognize that at that moment she still had a place to live. She could choose to give thanks and wait for God to answer her prayers for provision. Not only did she still have a place to live, she also had the basic necessities.

When you are able to present your requests to God

with gratitude for what you already have as well as for what you expect, his unfathomable peace descends upon you and keeps you in a state of sanity. In God's presence there is abundant joy, so in your moments of distress and anxiety, you need to cease from your activities and be still before him. There you can hear his directive on solutions and alternatives that may even annihilate the cause of your worry. You cannot hear him amidst the noise of your complaints and anxiousness.

Like the psalmist in Psalm 103:2, you can take time to appreciatively call to mind God's blessings, both tangible and intangible. Gratefulness empowers you and promotes well being and healthy attitudes, but failure to give thanks makes you feel powerless and victimized. Gratitude enables you to see how much you truly have, but grumbling focuses you only on what you lack.

Isn't it absurd how we get anxious about something that does not exist, like something that *could* happen next week? A future event exists only in the realm of your mind. Have you ever worried about something only to find that it turned out differently than you expected? Needless to say, the power of your imagination can bring it to pass. Isn't it a wonder that Paul encourages us to think on the things that are productive, positive, and praiseworthy?[26] Is it any wonder that Jesus says you cannot add an hour to your life, so you shouldn't worry about tomorrow?

How long must you hold out in faith? When Jesus' disciple, Peter, walked on water, he had confirmed with Jesus that he could do it. Seeing the high waves around him, however, he began to second-guess the confirmation. Anxiety had overcome him although Jesus hadn't changed his position in any sense of the word. It was Peter's human side, one might argue. Yet that is where we, like Peter, are challenged. How long can we remain in the place of faith before we revert to our human way of thinking? How much can you "do all things through Christ who strengthens you?" Before you can apply God's Word to your life, you must know and be willing to abandon the accommodations of our human tendencies. It is not automatic; you must press on. Faith takes work!

God instructed the Israelites to write the commandments and post them where they could see them all the time, so that they would remember them. I make that a regular practice too, for I do get distracted and am prone to forget. You can set written or recorded reminders to yourself to give thanks and resist the temptation to complain. Be anxious for nothing. Pray about everything. Give thanks for all that you have or desire. Those who know God's Word experientially have great peace and nothing easily offends them, not even impending foreclosure.

Dear Lord, please help me to turn those needless moments of anxiety into moments of praise and thanksgiving. Help me to monitor my thoughts and choose to think on the things that are true, honorable, right, pure, lovely, and of good repute. Please forgive me for not trusting you to take care of my life. Thank you for being with me and giving me peace. Amen.

Reflection on
What Will we Do Tomorrow?

How do you manage anxious thoughts?

Try this: If you have a cell phone that has a calendar or datebook, or if you have an electronic organizer, enter a reminder with today's scripture reference. Set it to recur for at least one month. Be sure to turn the remind feature on. When you receive the alert, read the words aloud.

Write the same verse on pieces of paper or sticky notes. Paste a copy by your bedside, and repeat it aloud at bedtime. Paste the other one on your bathroom mirror, and read it to yourself each morning.

Gratitude

You may say to yourself, "My power and the strength of my hands have produced this wealth for me." But remember the LORD your God, for it is he who gives you the ability to produce wealth.

—Deuteronomy 8:17–18a

You brokered a very successful deal for which you were handsomely compensated, and you pat yourself on the back for a job well done. Good! But did you remember to acknowledge God, knowing that it was he who gave you the skill and opportunity to succeed? It is not very hard to get carried away with applauding oneself for achieving a specific goal without the mindfulness that it is God who made it possible.

Some people think it is corny, but I am always enthused to see celebrities at award ceremonies expressing gratitude to God instead of having it lost in the fame and fortune of Hollywood. Acknowledging that all of our abilities come from God demonstrates our humility to the Power that is higher than our own.

Yet, apart from taking the credit, we sometimes become very territorial and exclude others as we attain new heights of success. By being ungrateful to those whose input has enabled our achievement, we are expressing ingratitude to God as well.

God urges us to remember him, that is, to consciously call to mind his faithfulness, love, and goodness and to thank him for them. It is he who made us and gave us our senses, talents, health, inspiration, and all else. Express gratitude to him, not as a requirement but out of a deep sense of acknowledgment for what the favor means to you and how your life and that of others can be positively affected as a result. He is pleased when we praise him wholeheartedly and sincerely. When we give him credit for the things that we acquire, accomplish, receive, and enjoy, he blesses us.

How else do we say thanks or remember him? By giving back in tithes and offerings, sharing our time, self, and substance with others, taking care of the poor and the sick, singing songs of praise, testifying about what he has done, and so on.

Have you ever been praised for doing a good job? Picture this: You are a parent or mentor sitting in the audience at a prize-giving ceremony when your child takes the microphone and, calling you by name, proceeds to talk about your contribution to his or her accomplishment. In the presence of an entire audience, you are made to feel regarded, appreciated, honored, and significant. That, I believe, is a faint resemblance to the delight that God feels when we testify of how he enables us to accomplish anything—be it a small salary or great wealth. He made us to worship him.

It is neither by our might nor by our power, but by his spirit that we are able to accomplish anything.[26] The children of Israel gave what was known as thank offerings or built memorials to honor and celebrate God's goodness. You can create your own ritual of giving thanks. One way to do that is by writing a daily list of three or more things for which you feel grateful—literally naming your blessings one by one as the old hymn says. Why don't you start that today? Be thankful in all circumstances, for this is God's will for those who belong to Christ Jesus.[27]

> *Lord, your Word sets out the guidelines by which I should live. Thank you for reminding me of my obligations as your child. Let me never fail to acknowledge your acts of mercy and kindness. Accept my offering of praise and thanksgiving, I pray. Amen.*

Reflection on
Gratitude

Write down at least three things that have ever brought you financial gain.

1.

2.

3.

How will you acknowledge God for the specific skills or abilities you used to accomplish them?

How can you make a practice of "remembering the Lord" on a regular basis?

Incentives For Letting Go

"Good teacher, what must I do to inherit eternal life?" Jesus looked at him and loved him. "One thing you lack," he said. "Go sell what you have and give to the poor, and you will have treasures in heaven. Then come, follow me." At this the man's face fell. He went away sad, because he had great wealth.

—Mark 10:17b, 21–22

The rich young ruler in the gospel was devout in keeping the commandments. In his theology, wealth constituted the blessings of God, and so he came with an excitable countenance, perhaps expecting Jesus' approval. Well, Jesus acknowledged his earnestness and wanted to have him complement that outward conformity to the Law of Moses with obedience to the law of love.

Jesus' response could well have been, "How badly do you want eternal life? How willing are you to transform your way of thinking?" And so he drove straight to the heart of what mattered most: the man's possessions. The wealthy young man failed to see what he would get in return—"a hundred times as much in this life" plus "treasures in heaven." As earnest as he was, he could not see God's favor of eternal life worthy of the sacrifice of his assets.

Wealth must have provided a sense of security, power, and fame, all of which probably made him feel esteemed in society and approved by God. Maybe he felt that detaching from them would impact his image and social status. The thought of having to part with his possessions or wealth reversed his exuberance the way a bright sunny day suddenly becomes overcast with rain clouds. He was grieved and in deep sorrow when he left Jesus.

The story is told of Millard Fuller, a millionaire whose goal was to become a multimillionaire. Like the story in today's text, he had one problem, great wealth, that was getting in the way of true love. In the face of marital crisis, he came to the realization that more than acquiring wealth was the importance of securing favor with God, starting at home. He recommitted to his wife, sold all of his assets, and responded to the call of God to give to the poor. He found a way to do this by building houses across the world for families who could not afford one. The organization now known as Habitat for Humanity International has built thousands of homes for people worldwide. Now, that is laying up treasures in heaven!

How much heavenly treasure do you want to secure? There are no maximums. We put money into our retirement accounts and build up what we call our nest egg. Although some of these funds are insured from loss, they are not necessarily shielded from inflation. Their value could decrease over time. Not so with the heavenly treasures into which Jesus invites us to invest. God expects us to use our assets for the advancement of humanity. When we die, we take nothing with us. Excavation of the three-thousand-year-old burial site of the famed Egyptian king Tut confirms this. Articles of fine gold, silver, and other precious metals including a golden fan that was supposed to keep him cool in his transition into the afterlife were found still there.

Your attachment to possessions can be so significant that the thought of parting with them seems like an impairment to your identity and worth. Jesus was not looking to bankrupt the rich young man. But as religious as he was, he didn't know God well enough to trust him. What are you willing to let go to allow your transformation?

> *Lord Jesus, when you came into this world, it was to give away your most priceless possession—your life—so that I could be transformed into your image. Of all the things I can acquire, let me have love and the willingness to share it in a limitless way. Amen.*

Reflection on Incentives for Letting Go

What is your most valuable or prized possession?

Imagine yourself as the young man in today's text being told to give it all away. What emotions are you feeling?

What about gift-giving? Do you give only to people who can reciprocate?

Are you able to give beyond what feels "comfortable," or do you always watch the cost?

What Is More Important?

Better little with the fear of the Lord than great wealth with turmoil.
—Proverbs 15:16

After all the wealth has been acquired and accumulated, all the successes achieved, and all prosperity attained, what else is there? Solomon, having enjoyed all of these benefits and more, concluded that there is nothing as worth securing as God's favor through our reverence and respect for him. Everything else, he says, is as transient, fleeting, temporary, and passing as the wind against your face.[28]

He doesn't say this to give place to mediocrity, sanction laziness, or encourage complacency, for we all have a mandate from God to be fruitful. Neither is it to inflict guilt on the one who has acquired wealth via reasonable, legal, and honest means. To me, it is not the choosing of little over great wealth that establishes favor with God, as both are equal in their propensity to either drive you away from him or draw you closer and bind you to him. It is right relatedness to him that matters.

Some, even owners of luxuries, have dared to argue

or even teach that the Christian walk is one distinguished by poverty, as exemplified by Jesus, because he borrowed donkeys for transportation and had no place to sleep. But if the owning of assets signified an economic status to be denounced, Jesus would have been partaking in the ungodliness of any man who lent him a donkey or anything else. The converse of that is what is really true. Jesus is the rightful owner of the donkey of which he made the man a mere steward. In the same way, he makes us custodians of all that we possess and he may choose to put us in charge of great wealth.

It is when we choose to see wealth, and not God, as the object to be pursued that we begin to court turmoil. For wealth is not the source or bringer of joy and happiness, neither can it deliver the perfect peace that God gives to those who love him. In fact, even when acquired by equitable means, it has the potential to generate chaos and confusion, excessive demands of time and energy, anxiety, stress, fear, or other negative circumstances, depending on your mindset. The way a person perceives money can challenge mental, spiritual, and physical health if one doesn't know its purpose and place and then conform to it.

The writer of this proverb knew well that turmoil can be associated with great wealth, and he also knew the peace that comes through fear of the Lord. And while a person with enormous wealth can do much to contribute to life in positive ways, without the inner peace that comes only from God, he or she might be better off with only a little.

If our hope is in this life alone, we are, of all men, most miserable, as Paul says. What we need is to understand that we are not the providers of our own strength.

It behooves us to acknowledge the Power that is beyond our own and choose to revere and respect the Giver of life—present and eternal—wealth, wisdom, and all things, and to allow his sovereign rule over our lives and pursuits.

> *Lord, you know our deepest thoughts and intentions. I confess that I have gone after more material things to give me joy and happiness, but how futile that is! Please forgive me and make me to always know that my satisfaction comes from you and you alone. Amen.*

Reflection on
What is More Important?

How do you describe a wealthy person?

Do you resist the idea of becoming wealthy? If yes, is it because you feel spiritually safer with little?

What traits, behaviors, qualities, etcetera, do you think wealth would bring about?

Is it probable that these tendencies already exist within you?

What's In Your Heart?

The one who received the seed that fell among the thorns is the man who hears the word, but the worries of this life and the deceitfulness of wealth choked it, making it unfruitful.
—Matthew 13:22

This parable reminds me of when my mom once planted two patches of peppers: one a few feet from our house and the other in the field about two miles away. They both sprang up nicely, but because domestic obligations kept her at home, she tended the one close by and not the other. Months had passed before she returned to the patch in the field, only to find a few "struggling" plants of peppers that were being crowded out by an overgrowth of weeds and briars. The overpowering nature of the thorns choked the unguarded peppers, hindering them from producing a crop.

The Word of God, when planted into our hearts, requires the same nurturing as a physical garden. We have the responsibility to guard it from worry, which, like thorns, is overpowering in nature. How do we guard it? Through studying and obeying God's directives. I believe that for every thought of fear and fretfulness, there is a word of faith and promise. We can use them to respond to anxious thoughts that enter our minds. Sometimes our own self-talk can challenge the truth that we are trying to believe. God's Word cannot return to him without accomplishing the purpose for which he spoke it,[29] so if we believe the word that we speak, it will do whatever he said it would. So just be persistent. If worry consumes us, there is no room for the Word to bear the fruits of faith. That is why God said that we should not worry.

It is not hard to get carried away with the things of this life, such as financial demands, job advancement, and so on. We call those things *reality*. But reality, as we know it, is our biggest hindrance to faith. Reality says, "But the market is bad, the bills are due, and the child is sick. I can't help being worried." Faith says, "What is not possible with man *is* possible with God. Be it unto you according to your faith."[30] We can practice speaking words of promise and encouragement to ourselves every day until they take roots and grow deeply.

But worry is not the only thorn that chokes the Word. The enticement of wealth can equally suffocate the spiritually weak and fragile. But what exactly is *the deceitfulness of wealth*? Does wealth have a nature? And doesn't the Bible say that wealth is a gift from God? How can it be deceitful?

Wealth does not possess a nature as humans do, so it cannot have animate attributes. The sense in which deceitfulness is used here is no different than saying that the piece of cake is tempting. But is it really? Does the cake have the power to make a person eat it? If it can tempt one person, why can't it tempt everyone? The answer lies in one's behavioral tendency toward an object like wealth.

Only humans possess the ability to be deceitful, i.e., by definition "given to cheating."[31] One can allow oneself to be so consumed by the power of wealth that he engages in corrupt practices to get and accumulate it instead of using it for its true intent—the material sufficiency of self and others.

The need to amass riches is undeniably the result of fear, stinginess, and lack of trust in God as your source. Nevertheless, these tendencies can all be overcome by meditating on the truth in the Word of God and making it your reality. Remember, wealth is temporary and can be lost. God's Word lasts forever.

Lord, forgive me for the times when I get enticed by money. Help me to meditate on your Word, and when I am tempted to trust in myself, let your presence and power surround me. Let me keep your words deep within my heart so that I do not sin against you. Amen.

Reflection on
What's In Your Heart?

What is the most fundamental aspect of your personal relationship with God?

How does that influence your inclination to worry or your ability to be expectant?

How can you strengthen or nurture this aspect?

How much of your prayer time is spent in asking and how much in praise and thanksgiving?

The Real Payday

Now listen, you rich people, weep and wail because of the misery that is coming upon you. Look! The wages you failed to pay the workmen who mowed your fields are crying out against you.

—James 5:1, 4a

The book of Proverbs speaks of a certain way that seems right to a person but ends in destruction. It could appear that some people challenge God and get away with it; they oppress the poor and exploit others—yet by all appearances, they are blessed and prosperous. Their apparent success can fool the weak willed, who may even abandon allegiance to God to indulge in wretchedness and greed.

The chase for wealth can desensitize employers who exploit their regular workers while awarding lucrative compensation packages to top executives. Very often, because they have little or no recourse, migrant and foreign workers, especially, are mistreated, poorly paid, and abused in unthinkable ways. But such perpetrators will not escape God's judgment. The Lord says that he will speak against those who cheat employees of their wages and deprive aliens of justice.[32] I was appalled to learn of a giant U.S. corporation paying customer service representatives in a so-called third-world country the equivalent of $2.50 per day *in 2006*!

You may reason that God is oblivious of these practices as you see persons or organizations going unpunished and their profits continuing to grow. But the psalmist says that God laughs at the wicked, for he knows their day is coming.[33] Maybe you are not taking advantage of others in a very big way, and you may even justify your actions by saying, "Everybody's doing it," or "I'm not as bad as those other guys." But don't forget that every individual is accountable to God for wrongdoings of any nature. Solomon, in the book of Proverbs[34] says that those greedy for riches set an ambush for themselves. These are lovers of money who have no fear of God and live for only the moment.

God is the all-time Defender of those who have been made poor through social or economic injustice and abuse brought on by systems and individuals with greater power. He demands empowerment of those needing justice and condemns those who refuse to do so.

No matter what your financial standing, if you have failed to pay those who render services to you or your organization, you are guilty and accountable. God, through his prophet Jeremiah, cries out against the one "who builds his house by unrighteousness and his chambers by injustice, who uses his neighbor's service without wages and does not give him his pay ... He judged and defended the cause of the poor and needy; then it was well. Was not [all] this [what it means] to know and recognize me?' says the Lord" Jeremiah 22:15.

The certain disgrace and humiliation that God predicts upon oppressors and extortionists prove that he is serious about responding to the cries of the exploited. In recent times, numerous media reports[35] of companies like Enron, confirm that justice will prevail. Choose fairness to your workers and in all of your dealings so that it will be well with you.

> *Lord, your eyes move to and fro throughout the earth, strongly supporting those whose heart is completely yours.[36] Please help me to remember this always, especially when I am tempted to hurt others. I commit to seek your help in difficult situations when my human frailties urge me to act in ways that do not testify to your righteousness and goodness. Teach me your ways, oh Lord. Amen.*

Reflection on
The Real Payday

How do you feel when you have to compensate someone for his goods or services? Does it ever make you feel as though you are reducing your financial power and that you can't hold on to money?

Do you ever get the feeling that you should be recompensed for prior losses, even from someone who was not responsible?

Even if you are not rich, have you ever deliberately held back your worker's wages or creditor's payment unnecessarily?

If you answered yes to any of these questions, how does that make you feel?

Hope Thou In God

Command those who are rich in this present world not to be arrogant nor put hope in their wealth, which is so uncertain, but to put their hope in God, who richly provides us with everything for our enjoyment.

—1 Timothy 6:17

The Word of God repeatedly warns us of the power of money to influence our devotion to him. Accumulated wealth can fool us into thinking that we do not need God. In fact, the wealthy have long had a reputation of arrogance, snobbishness, and self-satisfaction. But it is downright foolish for a person to put his hope in riches. One reason is that there is no guarantee about anything in this life. It takes only one moment for tragedy to topple a seemingly steady fortress. Lawsuits, natural disasters, health issues, and identity theft are only some of the events that can demolish one's acquisitions. What sense would there be to hope in something so fragile and subject to such vulnerabilities?

A financial advisor on the radio persuades his listeners to invest in precious metals versus currency, which, he says, is less stable. Yet even when we find the best vehicle for our investments, the truth of its uncertainty still prevails. There are many Wall Street stories of traders and investors who have ended their lives when the stock market saw a vicious downturn. The one whose hope is in money has no resilience or wisdom. Yet it is so much easier to place trust in the visible—wealth and possessions—than in the invisible—God. That is why hope in God is an act of faith, and it takes work.

Solomon teaches that wisdom is more profitable than silver and yields better returns than gold (Proverbs 3:14 (NLT). A wealthy man himself, with an annual salary of $25 million (U.S. equivalent) based his perspective on his possession of both wisdom and wealth. Doesn't that make his advice sound? What is the source of wisdom? It is trusting or putting one's hope in God, who never fluctuates. Those who rely on their wealth for happiness are disillusioned. In his study on suicide, noted sociologist Emile Durkheim found "higher suicide rates among the wealthy than among the poor," demonstrating that "industrial goals of wealth and property [are] insufficient in providing happiness."[37]

It is not the quality of your possessions but the quality of your spiritual character, your ability to persevere in the face of hardships—seeing them as instruments that test the integrity of your faith—that builds a solid foundation in *the life that is truly life*. If the object of one's hope is riches, and they should succumb to disaster, what would be left to hope in? But if your hope is in God and your assets suffer loss, be assured that he who gave them in the first place can restore them a second and a third and all subsequent times. And if he chooses to not do as you expected, know that God continues to be committed to you anyway. You need to be sensitive to what God is doing in your life.

God's intention for you is far greater than your intention for yourself. You can still count on his infinite wisdom because God has no plan to harm you. Trust him. God is not against riches or wealth.

If your hope is in God, he will give you wisdom to manage the affairs of your life. He will instruct you and guide your choices. If you are rightly related to God and should feel inclined to become reliant on or to seek security in your acquisitions, he can get you back on course if you allow him. Ask God to heighten your consciousness of any such tendencies and teach you to place your trust in him alone.

Lord, your Word says that if anyone lacks wisdom, he should ask of you who give liberally without judging. I ask for it here and now. I freely place my trust in you, for you never fail. Thank you, my Source and my Hope. Amen.

Reflection on
Hope Thou in God

Do you sometimes feel dread that you could lose all your investments or acquisitions?

How would you cope?

Do you think a financial catastrophe could cause you to end your life?

What do you think is the ultimate purpose of life?

As A Man Thinketh

For everyone who has will be given more,
and he will have an abundance. Whoever
does not have, even what he has will be
taken from him.

—Matthew 25:29

Yesterday, I heard a politician on the radio lamenting that his city could not afford a certain amenity. Tonight, my niece told me that she could not afford a movie ticket. What do they really mean? For one thing, the statement conveys no hope. I get the impression that there is no possibility that any of these things will ever happen. No matter how you say it, *I can't afford it* is one of the most negative statements we use, and yet is so socially acceptable.

I can't afford it is quite a fallback for the person who:

- has no faith to believe what he or she cannot see at the present moment.
- sees himself as unfortunate, disadvantaged, and "does not have it."
- feels safer to misrepresent the truth
- is being resentful or sarcastic toward someone she considers to be more fortunate than herself.

It is one thing to be destitute of wealth and material things, even those necessary to sustain life, but it is quite another to perceive or speak of oneself as being poor and without means. Considering that God has given us all that pertains to life and godliness the declaration of lack shuts out possibilities instead of opening options. Such a thinker sees himself as powerless and is inclined to not take responsibility for his well-being. Someone else must pick up his tab. He is a bankrupt thinker. "Even what he has will be taken away from him."

The mind that thinks in terms of wealth and prosperity doesn't think it can't afford anything needful. Rather, it looks to the providence of God and seeks to find how it can finance this or that.

Some people would rather claim "I can't afford it" because they fear being perceived as affluent. But affluence doesn't necessarily mean that one has a lot of money. Even among low income earners are people with a genuine air of comfort and contentment. They are more optimistic, healthier, and happier, for their hope sustains them and makes them see what is possible.

Still, the biggest reason is an affront to something that can run deep. This, I think, is the most damaging of any reason why someone will claim inability to afford something monetary. It is the kind that promotes self sabotage. Our emotions are very tied up in our relationship with money.

On the instruction of a money coach, a woman once listed all of the things that she had been finding unaffordable over the course of several years. They spanned very different price ranges and relevance. As part of the exercise, she was required to state the emotional cost or the disadvantage of getting the things on her list. To her surprise, "demons" started coming out of her closet one by one. For example, the real truth about her inability to afford her mortgage was not that she had no income, but that she no longer cared to provide housing for her delinquent family member. Just a few months after becoming aware of and admitting the truth, she found a job of her desire.

If you are willing to be honest and look deep within, you can find your own freedom to acknowledge that you *do* have. Then you can live abundantly and like the conqueror you were meant to be. You have the privilege and choice of reframing your beliefs to be centered in truth. Don't misrepresent God. Instead, affirm that he has given you all that you need for life, even in the moments when you don't see it. Ask the Holy Spirit search your heart and help you to overcome your fear. Yours is the prosperity and affluence befitting the children of the God who made the world and everything in it.[38]

> *Lord, please help me to remember that I have the power to manage my thoughts. I resolve to renew my thoughts constantly and be on the lookout for pessimistic beliefs that hold me back from what you intend to establish in my life. Thank You Lord. Amen.*

Reflection on
As a Man Thinketh

Draw two columns on a blank page. In the first column, write a list of six things you have said that you are not able to afford.

In the other column, write the downside (disadvantage) of having those things (For example, "I can't afford blinds for my windows." Downside: *If I saved up and bought the blinds, my wife could believe that I am not serious about moving from this house.*)

Once you have completed the lists, go back to Column 1 and try to identify whether you are making an excuse, perceiving yourself as poor, unfortunate, and disadvantaged, or sabotaging yourself.

Ask God to give you the courage to search yourself and to show you the best way to overcome.

Wealth With Wisdom

With me, [Wisdom] are riches and honor,
enduring wealth and prosperity.
—Proverbs 8:18

I believe that if there is ever a formula for success, it can be found in the book of Proverbs, and particularly chapter 8. One of the "wisdom books," it gives instructions on how to avoid the pitfalls of folly and live a holy, happy, healthy, successful, and prosperous life. Its primary theme is wisdom, and the first step in attaining it is in fearing the Lord.

But what is the fear of the Lord? It is having profound respect and reverence for God, our Ultimate Authority. It is in knowing him intimately (through dialog with him and by reading his Word, the Bible), and wholeheartedly trusting his principles. A person who refuses to fear God is a fool,[39] which means that he or she is morally deficient. The dictionary also defines a fool as one who is regarded as deficient in judgment, sense, or understanding.[40] The scriptures further states that "fools despise wisdom and discipline."[41]

Wisdom is found in studying the Word of God, which covers more subjects than most of us are aware.

We can count on its guidance on matters for which we need counsel or assurance. Wisdom guides our decisions like the one I had to make some time ago when a family member asked if I could use my credit card to purchase a "big ticket item" for her. Inasmuch as I desired to be nice and helpful and secure her admiration, I chose to follow biblical advice to not guarantee another person's debt.[42] It was not easy to do, but, because I had experienced the consequences of similar nature in the past, I was not prepared to lend what I could not afford to lose. James teaches that any person who knows what is right to do but does not do it, to him it is sin.[43]

The Word of God has some of the soundest principles regarding money, credit, spending, and saving. I wish I had known that "it's safer not to guarantee another person's debt" and that "it's poor judgment to guarantee another person's debt or put up security for a friend"[44] before I cosigned with some of my friends several years ago. On the three occasions when I did this, I ended up having to pay off the balances, thereby ruining our friendships, my credit rating, and my own financial health.

Wisdom guides us to delay purchases that we have not budgeted for instead of gratifying ourselves in the moment and risking our futures in the process. Wisdom leads us to seek God's guidance and sustains our ability to wait on him. It instructs us to seek expert counsel on matters in which we are not informed enough to make decisions. When we practice to pray and meditate, God meets us and shepherds us in the ways that make our lives more successful and prosperous. We can spare ourselves pain and loss and be more fulfilled if we cease to rely on our own ideas and opinions and instead use the greatest resource ever—the Word of God—to instruct us in wisdom.

There is a difference between the wisdom of man and that of God. If we allow him to transform us, he will conform our ways to his. The person who seeks wisdom in the course of his life will be rewarded with riches, honor, enduring wealth, and prosperity. Wisdom enlightens us that true wealth is not the kind that moth and rust can destroy or that thieves can steal.

> *Dear Lord, so often I rely on my judgment and neglect your wisdom to guide my choices and decisions. But how they lead me astray! Help me to trust you more, for you care about me. Let me be so self-controlled that I will not make hasty decisions even when it seems like you are being slow in your communications, for your Word says that none who wait on you will ever be put to shame.*[45] *Amen.*

Reflection on Wealth with Wisdom

How do you tend to respond when someone asks you to help them to "establish credit," cosign a loan, or make a purchase that is beyond your current budget?

Are you concerned about how you will be regarded by him or her?

Are you concerned about how others will look at you if you turn down their requests for monetary favors?

In making decisions, are you inclined to be guided by the Word, your opinion, or society's standards?

The Habit Of Gratitude

Be thankful. It is a good and delightful thing to give thanks to the Lord.
—Colossians 3:15; Psalm 92:1 (AMP)

It is so easy to find things about which we are dissatisfied: our jobs, the bills, the traffic, the political system, the weather, the members of our household. You can tell that I've expressed quite a bit of dissatisfaction myself! But the thing about complaining is that it saps energy and blocks creativity. Over the years, I have become more keenly aware of my tendency to look for what is missing in my life instead of being grateful for what I do have.

Before I started learning to relate positively to money, a sense of remoteness existed between it and me. Very often, whenever I received it—whether as a gift or compensation—I would see it as "not mine anyway," so I never paused to acknowledge its ability and power to bring the things I needed into my life. "I can never hold on to it," or "Money always slips through my hands," I would complain, instead of thanking God for sending it to me. In time, I started learning to be grateful for as little as the penny I found in the street.

One day I was paying a large bill with money that I had received only a few hours before. As the agent counted the cash, I felt an unfamiliar exuberance as I contemplated "the magic of money." Instead of the usual whining and complaining about parting with it, I felt a deep appreciation as I watched how the money worked to secure my necessities.

Have you noticed that Jesus had a healthy habit of giving thanks? Whenever he brought that attitude to what had seemed insufficient or impossible, something extraordinary happened. One example is when he fed over five thousand people with five loaves and two fish (Matthew 20).

Sometimes, though, it is not our lack of gratitude, but our nervousness and insecurity that interfere with our capacity to be grateful. We pay more attention to the half-empty than the half-full glass, to borrow the well-known expression. This was the perspective of the servant who was given one talent of money according to his ability to increase it.[46] His lack of optimism dulled his vision and impeded his outlook.

Ingratitude can cause you to look down on your assets and resources, especially when they appear to be smaller than you expected. If you see yourself as having nothing, even the little that you have will be taken away. On the contrary, those who perceive themselves as having more will be given "an abundance."[47] A friend told me that what you focus on expands. Your disposition regarding what you have will determine your success.

Do not resent parting with your money. It is designed to be circulated. When you hold on to it, stagnation occurs and your money fails to show a return. On the other hand, as you allow it to "flow" you receive materially and spiritually. Be thankful for the goods and services that it brings to you and others.

When you complain, more causes for complaining show up. When you give thanks, more causes for gratitude show up. Stop complaining and start giving thanks.

Dear Lord, I thank you for the money I have. I acknowledge that all things come from you. Help me to deliberately look for the things in my life for which I can be grateful. And in those difficult moments when all I can think of are the things that are missing or going wrong, please cause me to remember to take stock of what I already have. You are the Source of all that I need, want, and desire; and you care for me. Thank you, Lord. Amen.

Reflection on
The Habit of Gratitude

Do you feel resentment or other negative emotions whenever you have to pay bills? Why?

Recall a time when your bank balance was noticeably reduced. How did that feel? Did you impulsively start to consider ways to replenish it?

Do you consciously express gratitude for the goods or service you credited?

Review your telephone, electricity, or water bill. Bring your awareness to what they provided for you.
Give thanks.

Riches Without Godly Wisdom

A man who has riches without understanding is like beasts that perish.
—Psalm 49:20

One thing that I can remember about the rich families around whom I grew up was what I perceived to be their overwhelming arrogance. For that reason, I resented them. They spoke down to those who were not in their social class and acted as though they were gods worthy of worship. Years later, when they lost most of their resources, there was not a humbler family in town!

Howard Dayton, in his book *Your Money Counts,*[48] candidly shares the self-importance that he tended to feel whenever he drove his expensive car, admitting that "wealth stimulates deceit." That is the theme of Psalm 49 in which the writer calls out to the vanity of the wealthy who lack understanding, i.e., godly wisdom. To reject God, his offer of eternal life, and his ability to do all things, and instead rely on the power of riches is to be wise in one's own eyes. Godly wisdom opens up the desire to reveal the true essence and real nature of things and their deeper function in the ultimate purpose of God.

Some people misconstrue the value of money, thinking that it has use beyond this earthly realm. In this regard, they suppose that it will earn them the favor of God in the same way that it gives them esteem among humans. Therefore, possessing massive amounts of it and being able to do charitable works with it will offer exemption from submission to God's laws. What lack of understanding! The ransom for a life is costly. Verse 8 of our text says *no payment* is ever enough. God gives his approval only to those who recognize that they have fallen short of it and accept it through humility—acknowledging utter dependence on God for salvation. We can inherit the kingdom of God only with the childlike humility that the Bible teaches.

Growing up, I used to hear a popular song about how hard it is to be humble, but we can begin to develop that desirable characteristic by expressing gratitude to God as well as to the people in our lives and by being aware of our own mortality. Humility is not humiliation. In fact, it takes a lot of courage to be humble. If your wealth—real or perceived—has made you feel superior and caused you to treat others in a condescending manner or made you feel godlike, you need to rediscover your mortality. That would indeed be godly wisdom!

Paul advises us to subdue the impulses of the flesh, which is the seat of the ego, for it glorifies the self and other created things instead of God. The ego is the element of the flesh "in control of the will which must choose between the law of God and the lawless desires of the flesh."[49] The flesh, in fact, wars against the spirit, and when the flesh wins, our spirituality suffers and we become perishable like beasts.

God has no desire for any of us to perish and that is why he gives us himself—his eternal immortal self. Since we all have access to this Infinite Gift, I can only encourage you to accept him and let him infuse you with his wisdom and understanding. As your relationship with God deepens and expands, you lose your desire to lean on your own understanding and instead come to rely on his ability to guide you along the best pathway for your life. Ask him for understanding in all areas of your life, and he will give it to you.

> *Dear Lord, I do not want to be like beasts that perish. Give me wisdom, knowledge, and understanding to embrace the true meaning of the life that will last forever. Help me to see how transient money is. I put my hope in you, Infinite One. Amen.*

Reflection of
Riches With Godly Wisdom

Would you say that you possess godly wisdom?

What assures you that you do?

How do you include God in the financial aspects of your life?

Do you submit all of your financial decisions to his scrutiny?

Did You Ask?

You do not have, because you do not ask. Ask,
and it will be given to you.
—James 4:2; Matthew 7:7 (NASB)

Psychologists say that the way we interpret life in our formative years influence the beliefs and behaviors in adulthood. For many years I struggled to believe that God would grant my petitions. Ever since that incident in my early teens when I asked him to spare me from an imminent whipping and he didn't, I failed to put him in charge of things that I could not control myself. I had gossiped with a friend about a girl whose mother threatened to report me to my dad. I prayed hard, "Please don't let him find out." When I was made to suffer the consequence of my actions, I blamed God and neglected to ask him for much; when I did ask, I was already sure that he would never answer.

Maybe you can identify with me. Instead of asking God, you have depended on your own efforts and reasoning to guide your choices, taking the way that seems right. At other times you may have conformed and have petitioned him, but have not always gotten your desires. Some have reasoned that this happens because God is not a genie who does your bidding at your command. Others have said that it is because God answers by saying yes, no, or not yet. While I accept these ideas, they don't always apply. Let us review another reason why we may not have received our requests.

Jesus says in Mark 11:24 (NIV) *whatever you ask for in prayer, believe that you have received it, and it will be yours.* We do ask, sometimes fervently, but what we fail to do is believe. The classical writer Andrew Murray[50] comments that when we pray, we "should be on the outlook for the answer [to our petitions] ... waiting and ready to receive them." Believing that you will receive completes the process of asking. But believing is neither automatic nor easy. Our attempts at it often get obstructed by suggestions from our own minds that we will probably not have what we ask for. This is called doubting, which is often evoked by fear, memories of offenses that have not been pardoned, our inability to see how our request will be facilitated, self-judgment, feelings of unworthiness, and many other things.

James in chapter 1:5–6 encourages us to ask of God. "But when [you] ask, [you] must *believe* and *not doubt,* because *he who doubts ... should not think he will receive anything from the Lord.*" The cause of the doubting must be identified and addressed, not brushed aside casually. Once you've cleaned up these issues, the act of believing can occur without the bombardments. "If our hearts do not condemn us, we have confidence before God and receive from him anything we ask."[51]

I have now come to prove that God is faithful. He is a friend who invites us to come to him with our anxieties, and he will take care of us in whatever way we need, according to his will. It is this assurance that allowed me to open up and tell him honestly that I did not trust him altogether. He comforted me and healed what psychologists call "the wounded child" within. God is not as committed to giving us what we want as he is to giving us himself and molding us into what he wants us to be. Why not take the liberty to ask trustingly? Ask. Believe that you will receive, and you will have it.

Heavenly Father, you have assured us that you will give good gifts to your children when we ask. We can only believe that by faith, especially as life on this realm appears more real. But you say that when we are as trusting as little children, we simplify the process of believing what we have not seen. It seems that the primary objective of this life is to train us to relate to you whom we cannot see. Only you can bring us to that place. Help us to overcome doubt and to accept that with you, all things are possible if we just believe. Amen.

Reflection on
Did You Ask?

Do you have at least one specific need that is not being met?

What do you suppose to be the reason?

In the context of today's study, what has been the quality of your asking?

Can you put into words exactly what you have been expecting?

Why not make that request again today and give thanks the way you will when you receive it.

Creative Survival

I tell you, use worldly wealth to gain friends for yourselves, so that when it is gone, you will be welcomed into eternal dwellings.
—Luke 16:9

One of the things that stands in the way of our success is inaction. "I'll pray about it" is a common excuse we use for not taking action. I do not say this with disregard to the power and miracle of prayer; however, we sometimes use it as a front for laziness, procrastination, and cowardice. There is a time to pray and a time to act in response to practical matters.[52]

In the story of the shrewd manager in Luke chapter 16, Jesus taught a lesson on the benefits of good judgment, comparing the mentality of the children of this world with the mentality of the children of the light. He commented that nonbelievers are sharper than believers in dealing with real-world scenarios. Jesus was not applauding or promoting dishonesty. On the contrary, by observing the man's wit, he reinforced the need for God's people to make smart choices, to be more honest about ourselves, and to take more risks in working through the circumstances that life presents. It is better for us to be astute instead of being sanctimonious, passive and complacent, and dishonoring our abilities to think in practical ways.

In the story, the lax employee, at risk of losing his job, quickly assessed his situation and so devised a strategy to solve his dilemma ("I know what I must do to make sure that when I leave, there will be people to give me a house and a home.") He executed his strategy instead of remaining passive or indulging in self-pity. His proactive approach won him goodwill, approval, and profit.

When Mary Kay Ash faced the adversity of discrimination against women in a direct sales company where she worked, she refused to pity herself and let her reality retard her. Instead, using her ability to sell, she launched out to found what would become the largest direct-sales cosmetics company in the United States, Mary K. Cosmetics, Inc. Another woman, Dorothy White, founder of Miracle Services Inc., created her own source of income when her husband, the family's sole breadwinner, became too ill to work. Being a shrewd thinker, she drew on her cane-cutting skills to launch a thriving housecleaning business. These two women refused to shrink back from their adversities or offer excuses for their limitations and instead took Jesus' prompting to be sharp-witted and proactive in creating opportunities.

You may not see how you can move on from where you are, but you can start by being frank about what is. From there you can begin to take small, simple steps to your own creative survival. So pray about it, but take some action also. Waste no thought in what should have been. Take pen and paper and jot down one skill, talent, resource, or asset that you have, big or little, and then ask God to show you what you can do with what you have. He will answer, and you will be wise to do whatever he says.

"The master praised the crooked manager! Why? He knew how to look after himself ... I want you to be smart in the same way—but for what is right—using every adversity to stimulate you to creative survival" (Ref. Luke 16:8-9, The Message).

> *Lord, help me to not let self-pity or excuses hinder me. Amidst adversity are opportunities for fulfillment and advancement. Open my eyes to see them and my heart to trust you. Teach me how to be astute in practical matters, I ask. Amen.*

Reflection on Creative Survival

Are you currently encountering a specific challenge or hardship?

How does it make you feel?

What actions could you take to bring about a change in your circumstance?

Have you done all that you can do to change your circumstances?

Are you able to visualize an outcome? What does it look like?

The Poor Among Us

Lazy hands make a man poor, but diligent hands bring wealth.
—Proverbs 10:4

I do not believe that all poverty is a result of laziness or negligence. Some economic, political, and social systems create the circumstances of oppression and impoverishment. But outside of such conditions, many individuals bring about their own dire states of want.

When one thinks of the term *laziness,* the picture of someone being lackluster or sitting idle and doing nothing is likely to come to mind. But did you know that even an energetic person busying himself in an occupation for the usual eight hours each workday could be classified as lazy? You probably know someone who is always broke or lives on a small salary and has the wherewithal to progress but makes one excuse after another for not advancing. That person could be *mentally lazy*! I was for a long time too, and it was bad news when I became aware that I did not lack the ability to pursue my dream. I was simply too lazy to find the way to do what it required. To me, it was easier to continue in the same mode, even though it was neither fulfilling nor meeting my economic needs and desires, than to venture into the unknown.

I have heard many times that the rich should give to the poor so that the wealth gets evenly distributed. Here is the concern I have with this: Will distributing the wealth change the condition of the poor? If apathy is the cause of that person's status, would one be serving his or her best interest to simply dole out money?

You have probably heard this proverb by an unknown author: Give a hungry man a fish and he will eat for a day; teach him to fish and he will eat for a lifetime. This goes to say that if a person can be inspired to discover and use her talents and gifts, she can become a productive and self-reliant citizen. People are not poor necessarily because they lack opportunities, but because they fail to do the mental work required to change their circumstance. Stepping outside of what is comfortable or safe takes effort. It is much easier to continue doing what we always do, and to follow the same routine day after day, than it is to create and stick to a new goal. But you can do it.

Successful people surround themselves with like-minded positive thinkers. They also seek the advice of experts in their fields. If your desire is to become a barbershop owner, your best advice is more likely to come from a dentist who has owned a business than your best friend who is afraid of taking risks and has no background in entrepreneurship.

If you desire to move to a place of plenty, then take some time to consider the activities in which you engage on a daily basis. Now take a look at the ones that you constantly put off and ask yourself, "Are my tasks producing something of worth to me, or are they just filling up the hours of my day?" The Bible warns that "a little sleep, a little slumber, a little folding of the hands to rest and poverty will come on you like a bandit."[53] Diligent hands bring wealth.

> *Dear Lord, in speaking to Adam and Eve, you said, "Be fruitful."[54] Help me to not be afraid to take the steps to advance, for I recognize that it is not enough to simply dream. I want to be an effective human being, making a worthwhile contribution through the work of my hands. Amen.*

Reflection on
The Poor Among Us

In your current employment, are you utilizing the best of your abilities, gifts, or passions? (If unemployed, consider your last job or one that you are pursuing).

What is hindering you from moving to the next level?

What small step could you take toward overcoming this?

When can you start?

Job Satisfaction

When God gives any man wealth and possessions and enables him to enjoy them, to accept his lot and be happy in his work—this is a gift of God.
—Ecclesiastes 5:19

I said, "Wow!" when I first read this verse. To learn that God cares that a person has the ability to not just *have,* but to *enjoy* wealth and possessions, *accept* her purpose, and most of all, be *happy* in her work made me feel as though I had discovered a secret about him that few have ever known. I had never before considered these earthly things to be gifts from God. In writing this book about money, I had often wondered whether I shouldn't rather be focusing on more "spiritual" topics like holiness, prayer and fasting, evangelism, and so on. But it is now very clear that the subject of money, wealth, possessions, and work is no less important to God and is vital to our spiritual nurturing and growth.

Are you realizing the benefit of the things you own, or do certain situations keep you from being able to "sit back, relax, and enjoy" them? Does your conscience free you to take pleasure in them? Do you feel undeserving or guilty that you could relish the things that you have honestly earned? Does fear and anxiety make you feel insecure about their ability to last? Dwelling on these negative emotions can threaten or disrupt one's peace of mind, but frequent and genuine expressions of gratitude to God can reassure you.

How about your current job? Do you spring out of bed with enthusiasm to face the workday? If you do, then you're probably like my friend who told me, "I feel very, very fortunate to have a job that I truly love." This is enviable. A newspaper article cited a survey which showed that more than 25 percent of workers are dissatisfied with their jobs.[55] Are you one of them?

Before I discovered my purpose, which is to educate and enlighten others, I vowed that I would never take another job simply because it provided an income. I wanted to be happy in my vocation, but I wasn't clear about what God intended it to be. I spent time talking to him about it, borrowing the words of the psalmist in chapter 31, "Since you are my rock and my fortress, for the sake of your name, lead and guide me." Having that clarity now, I use my love of writing and teaching to earn a living and to live my purpose.

It is unlikely that a person will enjoy wealth and possessions if he is not happy in his work or at least some aspect of it. It is possible that every job that a worker hates is the dream that someone else is trying to find. If you enjoy yours, give thanks. If you don't, you may want to establish whether or not you are pursuing your calling. You may end up giving up certain conveniences, but in the end, you could be more fulfilled, happy and at peace. More than simply having wealth, possessions, and work, it is the ability to enjoy them that is a gift from God.

Do an assessment of your level of comfort about your wealth, possessions, and work. If you are not able to take pleasure in them, know that it is your responsibility to find your own comfort and happiness. Make a commitment to look at what you are not enjoying, what is missing, or what you desire at a deeper level. Resist the tendency to blame anyone or make excuses. Take the bold step of making the needed changes. Only then can you hope to get pleasure from the gifts that God has seen fit to bestow on you.

Lord, I am excited to learn that you care about these aspects of my life. I dedicate them to you so that you will be honored and exalted in my expression of your joy. Let me never settle for anything less than what you designed for me. Thank you Lord. Amen.

Reflection on Job Satisfaction

What have you acquired through your career or economic pursuits?

Are you able to enjoy your accomplishments?

What motivates you to carry out your current work responsibilities?

Do you find your work meaningful?

What does or doesn't make it so?

If you do not find your work meaningful, what would you like to change?

No Poverty Here

You will be made rich in every way so that
you can be generous on every occasion.
—2 Corinthians 9:11

The possibility of being made rich in *every* way is inspiring. It truly is the only way one can be generous on every occasion, the only way one can contribute on a large scale to the lives, dreams, and purposes of others. It is undeniable that the needs in our world are vast, and the more limited one's resources, the more limited the reach.

There was a period in my life when the total amount of money I focused on earning was "enough." The purpose of a job was to enable me to pay my bills.

I had not been a working adult for very long when my family started to call on me for help with one need or another. One weekend I worked outside of my regular job, and since I had not planned on this extra income, I decided that I would use it to open a savings account. No sooner had I decided to open a savings account than a family member called with an urgent financial need. Feeling obligated, I sent him the entire sum—only a fraction of what would have met his need anyway.

I became upset because I was unable to do both, not initially realizing that it would never be possible as long as I was going to adhere to the law that I had established for myself—the law of enough. That law was not going to support generosity or anything else, for that matter. Until I embraced abundance and started to live in the awareness that I am a conduit of God's benevolence, my frame of thinking was always lack, deficit, and self-centeredness.

Changing my way of thinking about the subject made me see that money is really not in short supply and I am privileged to receive it from God as he sees fit. It is he who promises to increase my resources in such abundance that I can give substantially on *every* occasion. I am not the source; I only have access to it.

The purpose of your being made rich is to meet your own needs and to contribute to the betterment of humanity. It is not for greed, hoarding, or stockpiling. You will be made rich—so that you can be generous with talent, time, goodness, financial resources, and more. This allows you to be effective in God's work and to assist others who desire to get out of poverty.

Many of us have been cultured to think that we cannot be spiritual beings and wealthy humans at the same time. But how can one who never experiences abundance be "generous on every occasion?" I am not referring only to physical riches here, for a person can have a large financial portfolio while being mentally poor. Such a person has not experienced true abundance.

God will make us rich; but we must first give to his work, not out of obligation or from a negative emotional place, but with joy and purpose. When we give, we receive so that we can give in even greater measure. Claiming that

"I do not ask for much, just enough," therefore, does not serve the greater good or the expansion of the kingdom of God. It doesn't even serve you.

> *Father, I commit my desires to you today and ask that you will help me to not seek after selfish ambitions but to humble myself so that you will lift me up. I thank you for instilling in me the desire to give. Deliver me from my hoarding tendencies, and free me from the sense of scarcity that sometimes overwhelms me. I ask it in your name. Amen.*

Reflection on No Poverty Here

Do you desire to become rich or richer?

Do you enjoy giving?

Can you identify specific persons, movements, or charities to whom you would be generous? If yes, in what ways?

Relating To Money

No servant can serve two masters. Either he will hate the one and love the other, or he will be devoted to the one and despise the other. You cannot serve both God and Money.
—Luke 16:13

One reason why people may be cautious about becoming rich is the fear that they will cease to give God the highest place in their life and will instead become enslaved by money. Being its servant would obligate them to work for this personified object, Mammon. I have learned, however, that one needs not be rich to be so inclined, for even the person in dire poverty can become preoccupied with money so much that he becomes like its hired servant.

God wants us to love him with our total being. But there is one thing that easily competes with God for power; it is money. Solomon declares that money is the answer to everything; the person who has an abundance of it can make almost any impossibility possible, to paraphrase William Shakespeare in the play, *Timon of Athens*. Because it possesses the ability to offer contentment and fulfill dreams, men and women have been deceived by the power of what Shakespeare in that play also calls the visible god. This god is very attractive to the one who seeks to fully control his own destiny such that there will be "nothing to worry about." It is also enticing to the one who seeks to have every desire fulfilled, no matter what the nature of it. In essence, such a person can create a god of money for himself.

Whomever you choose as your god will get your ultimate love and adoration. In true worshiping, our bond with our object of worship takes us to the point of trust and reliance on the power that is beyond ourselves. Clearly then, it will be one or the other, God or Mammon, that gets our devotion, never both.

So what does this say about possessing money? To be sure, money in itself is neither good nor evil. We all know it is something that we exchange for providing the needs of our lives: food, shelter, education, health, recreation, and so on, directly or indirectly. Jesus did not say we can't *have* money and serve God. He said it is not possible to be sold out on money—with the impartiality with which a slave serves a master—and still be sold out on God with that same level of dedication. "He will hate one and love the other," Jesus stated.

The *love* of money is the root of all kinds of evil. It violates the commandments to not murder, commit adultery, steal, lie, and crave others' possessions—behaviors in which those greedy for money often engage. These attitudes are based in the self and its desires, all of which will pass away. The love of God, on the other hand, is the source of every kind of good thing and is made complete when the genuine servants of God love him with all our hearts, souls, and strength (*all* meaning entirely, with nothing remaining) and also love others as much as we love ourselves.

Money does serve a wonderful purpose in our lives. In fact, my personal view is that our attitude toward it helps us to gauge the integrity of our relationship with God. Let us be careful in our handling of it so that it serves us in the fullest way as we allow God to be the master of our lives.

Lord, please give me wisdom to manage money well and in a way that gives honor and glory to you. Let me never get carried away by its power, which is temporary, but let my trust be in you alone. Amen.

Reflection on
Relating To Money

How can you tell if you are serving money?

How can you tell if you have been serving God?

How can you balance your love for God and your pursuit of money?

Would you say there is a healthy balance between God's place and money's place in your life?

How Should I Give?

In the course of time Cain brought some of the fruits of the soil as an offering to the LORD. But Abel brought fat portions from some of the firstborn of his flock. The LORD looked with favor on Abel and his offering, but on Cain and his offering he did not look with favor.
—Genesis 4:3–5a

When I first read this passage, I did not see why God accepted Abel's and not Cain's offering, as they both did what they were expected to do—bring their gifts before him. As I reread it, I noticed a very subtle distinction. The writer did not describe Cain's offering, other than saying that he brought *some*; but of Abel's, he said that the offering was the "fat portions of the firstborn of his flock."

There was obviously a difference in the quality of the offerings that each of these brothers presented to God. The term *fat portions* suggests a richness in quality—the best cut, so to speak. Because God did not look on Cain's offering with favor, could we suppose that his was just plain and second rate and not intentionally handpicked from the choicest of his field? And apart from the attributes of the gifts, could one detect a certain attitude with which each man presented his gift? Maybe Cain felt deprived to have to give his most valuable asset, while Abel felt fulfilled, believing that only his best was worth giving.

This text caused me to reflect on the quality of my personal gifts to God. Sometimes they are just plain and second rate, lacking willingness, gratitude, gladness, and commitment. Those include the times when I rationalize giving and justify why I can't afford it or perhaps why the church or other recipient doesn't need or deserve my gift. I may as well have kept my money or used my time or talents in different ways. If I offered them out of duty, thinking it would make me look good, but did so with grumbling or complaint, God did not look on them with favor. Cheerfulness must accompany my giving if God is to bless it. That's the only way I should expect to see "good measure, pressed down, shaken together, and running over."[56] With the same measure that I give, it will be given back to me.

How is the quality of your own giving? Do you grudgingly drop the smallest of the notes you can find in the offering basket, or do you delightfully and intentionally give a meaningful portion of what God has allowed you to earn through the blessings of health, skill, or whatever else made it possible? Does God look with favor at the time or talent that you give in service? Can he compliment you on being a good and faithful servant?

Giving out of guilt or duty will not bring God's blessing to us no matter what the size or frequency of the gift. Giving in tithes and offerings is an expression of gratitude to God who gave us the wherewithal to earn incomes. "You must each decide in your heart how much to give.

And don't give reluctantly or in response to pressure. God loves a person who gives cheerfully."[57] Just consider the approving attitude you have had toward someone who has expressed appreciation for your act of kindness toward them. It is that same spirit that you must have when you make your offering to God in order for him to look on it with favor.

> *Dear Father, sometimes I find it so hard to give. I recognize that the mentality of scarcity causes me to fear that my money will "run out." Help me to remember that you reward the faithful giver and that there is an abundance of money that I will never be able to exhaust. Amen.*

Reflection on
How Should I Give?

Recall a time when you were hesitant to give to a person, charity, etcetera.

What emotions did you feel (disgust, fear, guilt, etc.)?

What did you think being called on to give would have affected?

What was the outcome? What lesson was there for you?

The Best Part

Honor the Lord with your wealth and with the best part of everything you produce. Then he will fill your barns with grain, and your vats will overflow with good wine.
—Proverbs 3:9–10 (NLT)

I remember the basketful of freshly picked pears that the farmer brought—they were fit for a king, but they were for the headmistress of the local school. He and others demonstrated their appreciation of "respectable people" in the community by presenting them with the choicest produce from their first reaping. They gave the cream of the crop! That's what God expects from us—that we pay him tribute with our substance and with the best part of everything we produce, not with the leftovers or as an afterthought.

"What's in it for me?" you may ask. "Won't giving deplete my resources?" Well, look at the verse again. Honoring the Lord is paying respectful appreciation for him. It is giving him credit for what he has done for you. You see, God gives to us in terms of jobs, income, etcetera, and asks that we acknowledge him and express our gratitude by giving a portion back to him. When he receives that from us, he turns around and refills the store from which we gave. True, God shows mercy to everyone unconditionally, but those who honor him receive abundant outpouring as today's text tells us.

There is a miracle in giving, because when it is done with the attitude of cheerfulness and not fear, guilt, pressure, or hidden agenda, the giver ultimately receives more, not less. How? Suppose you helped a person in some particular way and some time later he returned to you with a gift saying, "I'll never forget what you did for me and want to express thankfulness in a tangible way." What would your disposition toward that person be? I bet it would be favorable. You probably would think of him when you see another opportunity that could benefit him, because he honored you.

In Levitical law, a tithe—which is translated as one-tenth or ten percent of everything that was reaped from the land, from the trees, or from livestock—was to be presented to the priests as an offering to the Lord. God promised that he would bring increase and abundantly bless the people who practice that principle, then and now. In addition, he pledges to preserve their crops from pestilence. That's better than any insurance plan!

I have noticed that each time God gives a command, he backs it up with a promise. Do that and I will do this. If you honor the Lord with your wealth and with the best part of everything that you produce, he will replenish your stock. Intriguing, isn't it? With this promise of increase, I am excited to give of the first fruits of everything I produce, and I do not have to feel embarrassed to think that there is something in it for me, for there is. Let me say that I am not giving because I want to receive; I give knowing that I will receive. It is an unchallengeable spiritual law.

Giving sometimes does not come naturally, but in those moments when you do not feel very inclined to do so, imagine yourself saying, "God, because you gave me the ability to earn this income I am expressing gratitude to you with this tithe and offering." This approach has changed the attitude and lives of many who have struggled with giving, and it can change yours too.

Lord, I confess that sometimes I am reluctant to give in tithes, in offerings, or in other ways. But I thank you for the promise in your Word that you will replenish my stock when I give cheerfully. You are able to make all grace come to me in abundance so that I will always be able to give to your good work abundantly. I commit today to honor you by cheerfully giving to those in need as well as to the community of faith. For Christ's sake I pray. Amen.

Reflection on
The Best Part

What are your honest feelings concerning giving and tithing?

How has this lesson influenced those feelings? Has anything changed?

Giving—It's A State Of The Heart

Each man should give what he has decided in his heart to give, not reluctantly or under compulsion, for God loves a cheerful giver.
—2 Corinthians 9:7

I was visiting a South Florida church, and when it was time for the offering, I considered giving one of the three-dollar bills I had in my purse. Reviewing the bulletin while I waited for the collection plate, I observed the church's three-year fund-raising projection of $3.5 million. In that instant, I withdrew my decision to make the offering as it seemed too insignificant against the huge projected sum. *My dollar will not make a difference to the goals or needs of this church,* I reasoned.

The thought had barely left my mind when the biblical lesson of the widow's mite[58] crept into my consciousness. She was a poor woman who, with limited income sources, had chosen to give all that she had—two small coins of little monetary value. Jesus, in comparing her with the wealthy givers in the temple, acknowledged the attitudes of faith and courage with which she gave, and for that, he honored her.

I knew there was a lesson here, and I paid full attention as God challenged me to be obedient to him and proceed with my giving. He wanted me to understand this often-slighted aspect of worship. No longer was it to be about making an obligatory offering to the church, for inasmuch as it needs my money, giving is not about the institution. It is about my personal ability to trust God and be obedient to him.

Giving is an act of worship, which not only benefits my spiritual health, but also testifies of God's faithfulness and love. It is tangibly expressing gratitude to him from a heart fully engaged and filled with joy and appreciation for the provision that he has made. It is from that very provision that he asks us to give back. Giving with uneasiness and anxiety about my means brings regret and heaviness of heart. This leaves no room for faith and growth.

"God loves a cheerful giver" is not just a cute saying. It has more truth and depth than some of us realize. It speaks about God, the Supreme Authority, bothering to love an act that we do with a certain spirit. The widow, in that spirit of intentionality and focus, would not be deterred by the size of her fellow worshippers' contributions. She gave from a place of faith—everything she had without holding back—trusting in the God who had provided those coins in the first place. How spiritually mature! She must have had a cheerful attitude, for Jesus admired her.

Wouldn't you want him to love the attitude with which you give? Have you ever found yourself grumbling or even sighing just a little when someone made a request of you? Have you ever questioned why the house of worship needs another fund-raiser, and even though you felt disgusted, you gave anyway? "God loves (He takes pleasure in, prizes above other things and is unwilling to abandon or do without) a cheerful (joyous, "prompt to do it") giver [whose heart is in his giving]" 2 Cor. 9:6–8 AMP.

If God is not going to approve of your giving, what's the point of it? Let the principles of love and cheerfulness—not guilt or duty—guide your decision every time you give.

Dear Lord, sometimes this aspect of my worship is marred by the demands of everyday living, selfish motives, and fear. These things cause me to hold back or to give sparingly. Infuse my giving with the gladness that you love so that it will be a true act of reverence. In Jesus' name I pray. Amen.

Reflection on
Giving—It's a State of the Heart

Next time, set aside some quiet time at home to put your offering in an envelope and bring a sense of mindfulness to the amount that you have decided to give.

Pay attention to the emotion that it is stirring. If you are not detecting a sense of cheerfulness, reread 2 Corinthians 9:7–12. Look for any feelings of hesitation, compulsion, anxiety, etcetera, and any discouraging self-talk, and ask God to replace them with true attitude of giving.

Free To Give

And God will generously provide all you need. Then you will always have everything you need and plenty left over to share with others.
—2 Corinthians 9:8 (NLT)

A pastor once asked me, "Why do people hold on to money?"

"They probably get a sense of security from knowing that they have it," I responded, based on my personal outlook and practice. I had always had a fear that my resources would run out and that my future would be dim. I had formed these perceptions when, as a child, I heard repeated warnings of authority figures saying that hard times were coming, and we were going to have to "bite the bullet." Thus, I always saw a future in which there would be hardship and never enough. For that reason, whenever I received money, I would try to hold on to it for as long as I could. Parting with it was never easy.

Even since I've started to relate to money in this more wholesome way, I have struggled with occasional feelings of fear and trepidation about an impending shortage. But as I continue to learn and grow, I become aware that scarcity is largely a mental conditioning. The willingness to renew my mind and affirm the truth that God will supply all my needs according to his glorious riches has given me significant triumph over scarcity. This assurance that Paul gave to the church for its generosity to him is equally true for you and me, and is based on the principle that if we give, we will not lack.

As true as the law of gravity is, so is the law of giving, which affirms that if you give, you will likewise receive.[59]

But giving *so that* you will receive is a means to an end, and is purely self-serving. God already promises that if we give, we will receive. There is a definite but subtle distinction here—one's motive for giving. The former is a game, but the latter conforms to the law of sowing and reaping—the assurance that there will be plenty. The Word of God is absolutely reliable and provable.

Have you ever heard the saying "Feel the fear but do it anyway?" In instances when this fear of scarcity takes hold of me, instead of denying or covering it up, I have dared to stand up and challenge it. Like David facing the giant Goliath, I let my conscious mind focus fully on that frightening belief that only keeps me powerless. Confessing my fear to God, I then affirm or meditate on the truth of God's Word that "he who supplies seed to the sower and bread for food will supply and multiply [my] seed for sowing."[60]

The truth sets you free when you speak it in the face of untruth. It sometimes takes many repetitions for a belief to become rooted, but with perseverance, you will get there.

I have hardly ever read this verse without feeling a sense of hope, excitement, and freedom—freedom to give and to test God in tithes and offerings, in sharing with the needy, in giving of my time, talents, and testimony. In those times when the little demon of fear of shortage raises its head, I confront it with this, or with similar truths of God whose lamb I am, and who ensures that I will never be in want.

> *Lord, I thank you for the good work that you have started in me. As I work to overcome this overwhelming fear of lack, I ask for your strength. Let me ever remain in your truth. As long as you are my Shepherd, I will never be in want. Thank you, Lord, for the liberty that is found in your Word. Amen.*

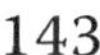

Reflection on
Free to Give

What generally motivates you to give?

Do you believe with sincerity that "God will generously provide all that you need?"

Do your present circumstances attest to that?

What do you do when you are tempted to fear that your needs will not be met or that giving will make you poor?

To Tithe Or Not To Tithe

"Bring the whole tithe into the storehouse, that there may be food in my house. Test me in this," says the Lord Almighty, "and see if I will not throw open the floodgates of heaven and pour out so much blessing that you will not have room enough for it."

—Malachi 3:10

For many years, I did not enjoy tithing, and spent time studying to find clarity on the subject and justification for my position on the matter. But I have learned that tithing is an act of worship, and an integral part at that.

Along the way, though, I have had to will myself to be obedient in tithing, especially when my expenses outweighed my income. On one such occasion, I struggled to the point of distress, and I wrestled with God. (Knowing the principles intellectually is never enough.) He lovingly led me to read, "He who supplies seed to the sower and bread for food will also supply and increase your store of seed and will enlarge the harvest of your righteousness."[61] That did it for me. How comforting to know that God is on this journey with me.

God expects us to prove him and his Word. In fact, he bids us to test him in tithing, and as every test produces a result, he urges us to anticipate something in return from him too. He will bless us abundantly above what we could ask or imagine, and he will shield our fruits from destructive forces. There's a good reason to tithe!

Tithing (one-tenth of our income) is not an isolated deed to win God's favor or blessing while one continues to live contrary to his teaching. He outright refuses that![62] Tithing and offering are acts of worshipful obedience to be done with utmost reverence and a clean heart.[63] Our tithe belongs to the Lord and is holy, and he says we rob him when we choose to not pay it. Furthermore, neglecting to tithe is an act of disobedience.

A radio disc jockey once polled his listeners to find out whether a person should pay tithe if all he or she has remaining is only enough to pay the utility bill. The popular response is that God is more understanding than creditors. That is absolutely true; however, creditors also have the disposition to extend grace. But I believe that in a well-managed financial plan, there is no toss up between the tithe and other obligations. Each has a valid place. In fact, it is because of the very understanding nature of God that he puts his reputation on stake for the faithful tither. He who fails to tithe robs not only God but also himself, for tithing builds and enhances one's spiritual health.

Managing our finances may call for us to reduce our cost of living, find additional or alternative sources of income, modify our spending habits, or streamline the distribution of our funds. As in all other areas of our lives, we must ask God for wisdom and courage and seek to educate ourselves in money matters. Jesus instructed his disciples to give to Caesar what belongs to him and to God what is his. But because God is unseen, it is easier for a person to behave as though he's absent. Only a deeper consciousness of God will make his presence and promises less abstract.

I have indeed proven that God will open windows of opportunity when I am faithful in tithing and offering, even in what they call "these tough economic times." I am so grateful for the income that he has provided that tithing has become a joy and is one of my means of saying thank you. If you struggle to believe that your tithing and offering will not bring you into a deficit, there is only one way to find out. Prove him.

> *The windows of heaven may open in a different manner than you expect or even have the capacity to imagine. In the stillness of your soul, develop your own intimacy with him and you will taste and prove that he is indeed very good. Lord, I want to prove you, but sometimes my faith is weak. Hold my hand as I take the step to trust you in my finances as well as other aspects of my life. Forgive me for those times when I failed to obey you in tithing and offering. Let me never forget that I am only a manager of your money, and you expect faithfulness from me. Amen.*

Reflection on
To Tithe or Not to Tithe

Have you noticed any shift in your views about tithing and offering?

God says, "Test me in this." Assuming that you have been tithing, in what ways have you been able to prove God? Write your testimony here.

Let God Be True And Every Man A Liar

You must set aside a tithe of your crops—one-tenth of all the crops you harvest each year.
—Deuteronomy 14:22 (NLT)

The pastor of a church I frequent led a series called the Law of Sowing and Reaping, in which he highlighted the importance of tithing. Not wanting to "rob God," I gave ten percent of all my income, expecting him to keep his Malachi 3:10 promise that he would "throw open the floodgates of heaven and pour out so much blessing that you will not have room enough for it." He did—or that is how I interpreted it—by causing the two-week contract on which I was working to be extended for an unexpected ten weeks! I felt fully assured that God would multiply back to me as I continued to tithe and that I would never again be out of money.

A little more than four months had passed since my last paycheck, and I now needed to understand why my store of seed had not been increased, and why this blessing had not been poured out in the measure that God promises. I decided to ask the Lord about it, since it was he who said, "Test me in this."

He responded immediately by telling me to look up the meaning of the word *blessing.* The first in the list of definitions that I read was *God's help.* I didn't stop there. I drilled for further evidence, so to speak. I found this meaning of the word *help*: "to make it easier or possible for somebody to do something that one person cannot do alone by providing assistance."[64] The first thing that came to mind was the wealth of support I had gotten in preparing this manuscript. The loving mentorship I received on relating to money was further demonstration of the word *help,* which is "to provide somebody with advice, directions, or other information."

When I started to count my blessings, as the old hymn[65] suggests, the wealth of solicited and unsolicited contributions in different areas of my life from friends, colleagues, and family, made me conclude that I was indeed receiving the blessings of God in abundance and in ways that I had not expected. These blessings included health, friendships, insight, coaching, and the list goes on and on. All I was anticipating was financial outpouring, but that's not all that God had promised, and he made sure to enlighten me on that fact.

It is true that God loves his children, and the thing that he commits to establish in us amounts to far more than I can ask or imagine. His ways are not our ways and we may be looking for certain outcomes, all oblivious to the things that God is pouring into our lives.

I believe that Jesus' goal to present us faultless before his Father makes him focus on our spiritual attainment more than the temporal. Yet this does not mean that he will neglect our earthly needs. Yes, he will increase my store of seed, but more so, he will enlarge the harvest of my righteousness when I am obedient and invest into his kingdom through the giving of tithes, offerings, and gifts.

God does not subtract from our resources without adding or multiplying back. The ten percent of our "crops" can be easily interpreted as an insurance premium, and God does not lie. We do not have to fear that he is like some of the unscrupulous insurance companies around. Put your faith to the test. Pay your tithe and see if he will not do what he said he would. Honor God with your money.

> *Lord, you are a faithful God! Your ways are past finding out. I thank you for your work of sanctification in my life. I am overwhelmed by your love and commitment, and when my eyes fail to see, you shine through my darkness with your eternal light. Because you are my Shepherd, I shall never lack. Thank you. Amen.*

Reflection on
Let God Be True

Have you ever felt as though God has not kept his Word to you?

What has today's meditation opened up for you?

A Growth Fund

Dishonest money dwindles away, but he who gathers money little by little makes it grow.
—Proverbs 13:11

In today's economy, it is not usually easy to find a worthwhile lump sum of money to save or invest. A vast majority of working people do express an inability to put away even a small amount from their paychecks. Some say that it is just something they cannot afford to do while others waste theirs away in frivolous spending. No matter what your situation, you are making an unwise choice in not consistently saving even a few dollars toward a financial goal. Many books, articles seminars, workshops, and systems are designed to teach budgeting and money-management strategies that are workable at any income level.

Some years ago, I met an office attendant who had just bought a new house. When I congratulated her, her eyes lit up with pride as she told me that for years she had participated in an informal cooperative that enabled her to save enough from her minimum wage to make her dream come true. This system can help even the undis-ciplined to save with consistency and achieve financial objectives that would not have been possible otherwise.

Many workplaces have investment and retirement funds to which employees can contribute even a negligible amount. Their nest eggs have the potential for large sums, especially if they participate for most or all of their working lives. Those funds are usually invested into stocks, bonds, mutual funds, and similar income-producing instruments with the potential to grow. (I doubt that many of us participating in pension funds and retirement accounts know that these are biblical principles). Partners, "sou-sous" (informal cooperatives), and direct deposits are simple alternate steps toward increasing your net worth. Investments that accrue compound interest can grow even more rapidly.

Persons at different strata of society have taken dishonest means to accrue wealth. Some employees steal from their bosses, while some employers are the ones to cheat those who work for them. Suppliers shorten goods and services, bookkeepers embezzle funds, both rich and poor rob from each other. No matter what the means, however, God rules over injustice and makes everyone accountable for his or her choice. Conversely, he takes note of even the smallest effort that conforms to his standards and directives and rewards them accordingly. I would rather have a little that he approves than an abundance that he denounces.

Have you pursued or taken advantage of investment opportunities? Do you find yourself putting it off until your earnings increase or until you are able to save a bigger sum? My friend tells me that her mom always says, "Don't wait till you are hungry to cook." Maybe you can start your own investment club with family and friends if you are good at handling money, or you can discuss options with a licensed financial planner or expert and put a savings plan in place. Money gathered little by little and by honest means has the potential to grow.

> *Lord, it is amazing how you guide in all aspects of our lives through your Word. Thank you for instructing us to make wise decisions regarding our finances. Help us to develop the discipline of investing not just for ourselves but for our offspring as well. Amen.*

Reflection on
A Growth Fund

Are you inclined to be unfair in your dealings with others?

In what ways do you justify that practice or way of being?

What does it mean to you if God doesn't honor it?

If you work for a company that has a savings/investment plan, do you participate in it? (If self-employed, have you considered putting something in place for that purpose?)

How much do you save per month?

For Generations To Come

Man is a mere phantom as he goes to and fro; he bustles about, but only in vain; he heaps up wealth, not knowing who will get it.
—Psalm 39:6

This psalmist, taking stock of his life, asks God to heighten his consciousness of what really matters in life and to teach him to spend the balance of his life in a productive way. He recognizes that his life is transient and unpredictable and that he is expected to be faithful with his earthly possessions. (I suggest that you read the entire Psalm 39.) As inevitable as death is, most of us give less than a passing thought to the subject. Our day-to-day involvements can take our attention from the integral responsibilities—especially stewardship.

Not so long ago, my niece attended the funeral of her thirty-six-year-old boss, who she describes as having been "quite accomplished for a man his age." He had founded a health care facility with four campuses. Constantly on the go, he barely took time for himself, but his career had the success to show for it. "It all seems like such a waste," she lamented. "Now you see him, now he's gone." Who knows what lucky man will inherit this thriving business if his widow decides to remarry.

The Word of God instructs us to manage our possessions so that we leave an inheritance for future generations. An elderly gentleman died after many years of hard and very productive labor. He loved his family and had given to them abundantly. He also invested prudently. At his death, he had no children or spouse to inherit his possessions, but he had some of those same relatives to whom he had been generous. Unfortunately, he did not leave a will. Years later, after his family had spent a great deal of time in prolonged legal proceedings to determine how his assets should be distributed, they were awarded a sum that was hardly worth a good month's salary. So, from that perspective, all of that bustling about was truly in vain.

It wouldn't have had to be that way if the gentleman had taken responsibility and named an heir to his possessions.[66] Neither does it have to be that way with you. With a properly executed will, you can leave a legacy for your family, religious organization, school, hospital, or charity. This demonstrates how well you guard God's blessings to you. He has made you steward of these things, and he promotes those who manage them with faithfulness and integrity.[67] When you leave them to the laws of the land to figure and appropriate, you give up your right to decide who benefits, and you also reduce the amount that your heirs will receive after the applicable governmental and legal fees.

Some people entertain superstitious beliefs about what writing a will could mean. The most popular myth is that it will hasten death. For this reason, people of all ages and backgrounds die intestate every year. I encourage you to draw up a will no matter how little you own or how young you are, as long as you meet the age requirements that are in effect where you live. Death is sure, and failure to execute a will has never been proven to delay it. Even more importantly, you should make sure that your soul is eternally secure after all of your bustling is over.

Father, the thought of death can sometimes be scary, and maybe subconsciously I believe the myth that making a will can bring about my untimely passing. Please help me to be wise in governing the resources that you have given me. I now know that shirking my responsibilities can bring unnecessary stress to my family. Cause me to express love even in leaving my financial house in order, I pray. Amen.

Reflection on
For Generations to Come

Do you have a will?

If no, which of the following reasons keep you from making one?

- ❑ You do not own anything of significant value
- ❑ You think it will hasten your death
- ❑ You have no heirs
- ❑ The possible heir(s) that you identify do not deserve it
- ❑ You have never thought about it
- ❑ You do not believe in wills
- ❑ Other reason:

If you need help, who may you ask to help you in drawing up a will? (Attorney, religious, or community leader, etcetera.)

When will you get it done? (Specific date.)

The Cost Of Ignorance

The younger son got together all he had, set off for a distant country and there squandered his wealth in wild living.
—Luke 15:13

Do you know the old saying: "A fool and his money are soon parted?" Although the parable in today's text is about redemption, the analogy that Jesus used is very typical of people who have inherited property but have no skill in optimizing its best benefits. You probably know someone like the lost son.

But it is not only inheritance that gets squandered away. Millions of people get paid on Friday and are broke on Monday. On top of all else that may be going on with them, these people have no money-management skills. Habits ranging from excessive shopping to drinking, to drug use, to gambling, to misappropriating, to giving it away unwisely are all means of squandering. What, if anything, do you squander your money on? Do you engage in wild living? Do you max out your credit cards on consumer items and end up with installments that eat away your earnings?

We do not know the full conversation that went on

with father and son in this parable, but there is nothing to suggest that the son received any guidance on how to manage his wealth, and he obviously did not know its purpose. It is also clear that he did not follow the example of his father, who had acquired and governed his possessions well enough to be able to have a legacy that he could leave for his children.

Advertisements bombard us with *must-haves,* and those of us with a pressing need to "fit in" get caught in the trap. A lot of us—unlike the son in today's text—are not recipients of any kind of inheritance. Could that be because our parents so overextended themselves to creditors that they had nothing to leave for us? Are you following the same trend?

I once walked into a store that offered 70 percent off and an additional 10 percent off if I were to use my store card. I hate shopping, but could not resist the bargains. Many months later, I was still trying to pay a debt that I hadn't budgeted for, and it carried an interest rate of over 21 percent. The *huge discounts* had become a huge debt! That is squandering, which has the potential to run us into financial, social, and spiritual ruin.

We have a responsibility to learn money management and teach it to our children. This skill is not taught in schools, but is fundamental to the proper handling of what God gives to us. Advertisers and marketers are in business to make profits, and they make every effort to make us spend. But we must be our own advocates and see to our own financial, emotional, personal, and spiritual development. Many books are written on these subjects. Also, workshops and seminars are given to educate us in financial matters. Take a look at your spending habits and those of your family, and assess whether you are clear about the value and purpose of money. A good rule of thumb is to assess how your next purchase will change your life. What would happen if you chose not to buy it? If it will not bring a necessary and vital change to you, your family, or your community, then you probably do not need it.

> *Father, I need your guidance in every aspect of my life. Teach me how to apply the biblical principles to my life so that it will be more fulfilling. Heal the areas of my life that I try to fill with material things. Use me to leave a legacy for coming generations in every way I can, and help me to be an example of good stewardship. Amen.*

Reflection on
The Cost of Ignorance

What do you normally say to yourself when you receive money? (If you are not sure, make a conscious effort to notice it next time, and then resume this exercise.)

Do these messages that you give to yourself sometimes reflect negative emotions such as fear, anxiety, sadness, blame, and so on?

(If yes, write those specific messages below, and next to those messages, write the negative emotions associated with them.)

Do you habitually use credit to purchase consumer items that your income cannot cover? Why?

If you got a bonus or an unexpected sum tomorrow, what would you do with it?

What Shall We Eat?

People do not live by bread alone; rather, we live by every word that comes from the mouth of the Lord.
—Deuteronomy 8:3b (NLT)

On March 3, 2000, the *New York Times* published an article alluding to the massive growth of billionaires in recent decades. Only eight years later, there were reports of a worldwide shortage of food, an impending recession, and a myriad of other economic problems. Almost unanimously, the world panicked, asking, "How will we survive?" We had gotten to be self-reliant, drawing on our own resources to solve our problems, and then suddenly we felt helpless. The crisis, however, forced some of us to reach out to the Power that is beyond our own.

It is at intervals such as this that God steps in to teach us the lesson he taught the children of Israel as they journeyed through the wilderness: our human efforts are never enough to sustain us. As God caused them to feel hunger, they used one of the two choices they had. They looked to him for sustenance. He was deliberate in removing the material comforts from them to establish his divine purpose in their lives. Maybe that is what he is doing in yours too.

As he did to them, he tests your ability to trust him and to solidify that trust. The Lord also withdraws necessities from us to train us to depend on him. In our conceit we can tend to believe that we are our own gods. As one contemporary writer puts it, "We have allowed our roles and possessions to define our identities."

One of the reasons people hoard is so that they will not lose control. Being in want is painful, so we will do whatever we can to escape it, sometimes at the expense of others. Yet Paul, in his letter to the Romans, encouraged them to be patient in difficulties, and told the Hebrews to "endure hardship as discipline" because it is for their ultimate good.[68] Virtue is not found in our ability to create a life of ease and comfort, but in our ability to transcend the difficulties that threaten us.

Pain and misfortune, however, have the enduring purpose of developing perseverance in us. That is possible only by faith. This is why James encourages us to not resist adversity, but to consider it "pure joy" when we encounter it so that we "may become mature and complete, not lacking anything."[69] True security cannot be found in the things that we are able to stockpile. We are not our own shepherds, and God's will is for us to learn that he is our Source, and he desires for us to rely on him fully.

As any loving father disciplines his child, so does our Heavenly Father who loves us far more than we can ever imagine. When he removes the conveniences from our lives, it is not because he ceases to care or intends to destroy us. Rather, he is working true spirituality into us. He is giving us the opportunity to test the theories of miracles that we read about in the Bible. God is giving us the occasion to put our own faith to the test and to prove that his Word is reliable. Through it all, he gives us grace to endure and is always with us, helping us in our efforts to know him and to trust his promises.

Father, I confess that I have sometimes relied heavily on my abilities instead of seeing you as the Source of all that I will ever need or desire. Please forgive me and help me to refocus my attention on your authority and ability to keep me in every situation. Unless you, Lord, build the house, all my labor is in vain. I welcome your discipline and thank you for being with me always, my Provider, my Source, and my Strength. Amen.

Reflection on
What Shall We Eat?

What passages of Scripture do you live by? (Write each one below.)

Are there any current national or world events that cause you to worry about provisions?

How do you handle those concerns?

These Final Words

We often speak of our bills as though they are some unjust penalties imposed upon us. It's as though we had no part in their incurrence. One night as my husband begged God for the nth time to "extinguish" our debt, I started to feel as though we were hopeless victims in chains, with little hope. *Not again,* I thought, glancing at the electricity, water, gas, and mortgage bills over which he agonized in prayer. Just then, it dawned on me that our perspectives needed to change.

Firstly, we had already enjoyed the benefits of the amenities for which we were being asked to pay, so our creditors were not being unfair. Secondly, the negative attitude that we were having in our prayers defied Paul's teaching to "Be anxious for nothing, but in everything by prayer and petition with thanksgiving make your requests known to God. And the peace that transcends all human understanding will keep your hearts and minds."[70] We were not experiencing peace, for our consciousness was charged with disquiet and fear. In that state of mind, we could not enter into *thanksgiving* .

Placing the bills on the table in the kitchen where we prayed, I called my husband's attention to the fact that even though our obligations were unmet, the services were still available to us. That was worth giving thanks for, as well as the fact that the companies had found favor enough to extend credit terms to us. I expressed heartfelt gratitude to God for providing the money we already had as well as that for which we trusted him. Immediately, I began to experience a calm and deep inner quiet knowing that he who promised is faithful to keep His Word.

There is a difference between seeing ourselves as the source of our provisions and depending on God for everything. The things we agonize about most are related to money. *My God, My Money* is intended to have us examine our beliefs about money, its functions in our lives, how God sees money, and how we can relate to it in a wholesome fashion. Throughout this course, we have come to learn that money is not scarce—that if we cultivate a sense of freedom about it, money will not enslave us, and that when we share, it gets multiplied. Money can impede our walk with God, but it also has the power to draw us closer to him. Money is not evil. In fact, it is a gift from God.

My understanding of the mind of God is heightened each day, and one thing is evident: God loves us immensely and has the utmost desire for our best. His objective is not to make us rich or poor, but to use the circumstances of our lives to strengthen our bond with him.

During the course of writing *My God, My Money* I have enjoyed financial abundance, but I have also had some shortfalls. I had been expecting my idea of a miracle to happen to allow me to retain a real estate property for which I was in arrears. Getting to this final chapter, I asked the Lord, "Aren't you going to give me a strong testimony to end with? Aren't you going to turn things around for me so that I don't lose my investment?"

God seemed to shake his head in responding, "You don't get it, then, do you?"

The truth is, I did get it intellectually, but now I needed to experience it! I recalled the Sunday morning when I wrestled with the possibility of an impending foreclosure. Borrowing the words of Job (Chapter 1:21b), I had said, "Lord, you give and you take away. Take everything you like, but leave my mind intact." Yet, here I was lacking courage to accept what he was "taking away." The opportunity had now come for me to have my experience, and in accepting it, I realize that God left my mind intact.

So I do have a testimony: My mind is in excellent health, and with it I can do anything. By the ability to think, men and women have built pyramids, skyscrapers, jet planes, and the pencil they use to draw them. The same intelligence that had conceived the real estate business is still capable of doing it again—and even more! So instead of submerging myself beneath my losses, I open my mind to see what is possible, for I can do all things through Christ who gives me the strength. My success is not tied to one endeavor, and I trust God for a new and better idea, for all things come from him.

What God yearns for us to "get" is that the things over which we travail are not what this life is all about. When tragedy occurs, we demand to know why a loving God allows it. He welcomes our questions. When he was asked why the man in the New Testament[71] was born blind, he said it was so that the work of God would be displayed in the man's life. The man's blindness motivated him to use his faith to ask for healing. When he received the healing, he offered praises and thanks to God. This brought God the glory.

We know that it doesn't always work out the way we expect. And when it didn't for one particular woman, Joni Eareckson Tada, who suffered a tragic swimming accident in 1967, she engaged one of God's gifts, the imagination, to paint with a brush between her teeth. Was that intended to give him honor? It sure was. Not only that, but her dilemma has moved her to find amazing ways to influence the lives of thousands of families affected by physical disabilities around the world—further glorifying God.

Who wants to suffer hardships? We try to escape them by putting the majority of our daily efforts into securing the comforts of life, and when we get detached from our earthly belongings, we tend to follow the natural path into gloom. But those disruptions serve good purposes. We can see them as opportunities to build perseverance and spiritual vigor. When we do not cower or buckle under catastrophes, we strengthen our faith. This life is about attaining spiritual maturity through our daily encounters. The wealth, riches, and possessions are "throw-ins," not the compensation. They are the by-products, not the products of the walk of faith. Our faith is not so that we can *have,* but so that we can *be.* When we get this distinction, we cease to squirm when hardship faces us and we acknowledge hardships as the teaching aids in God's classroom.

Acceptance of God's sovereignty gives us peace. If hackers break into your computer and steal your identity and ruin your credit, if the stock market crashes and you lose your investment, if your house forecloses, if your purse or wallet gets stolen, it is not because God hates you and is out to devastate you. What you allow those things to teach you about who God is and what he is up to in your life is the point. Of all of the things that we will acquire, there is only one that we must have to please God: faith. There is no substitute for it.

What has this journey taught you? It is my sincerest wish that you have been enlightened on the subject of money and that your relationship to it has shifted in positive ways. I also hope that you have come to a greater understanding and appreciation of God. I encourage you to reread the entire book or parts of it. You will continue to gain new insights. Finally, please accept my sincerest gratitude for taking this journey with me. I am truly glad that you did.

If you have never established a relationship with Jesus Christ, I invite you to pray this simple prayer:

> *Dear Lord Jesus, I acknowledge my need for your saving grace. Please forgive me of all my sins and draw me into fellowship with you. I accept you as Lord of my life. Amen.*

I would love to hear from you. Please feel free to share your comments, testimonies, thoughts, and requests for prayer by writing to judith@mygodmymoney.com.

God bless you.

Why Worry?

I was up again in the dead of night
Fear wanted to put my faith to flight
Fear that I would not be able to pay
Fear that I would renege on what I always say,
That when doubts come bringing anxiety
I'd speak the truth of God's Word to the adversary.
For the Truth is the only thing that can set me free
To resist the devil, yes, and make him flee.

My Father says to me, "Child, do not worry
About your life, what to eat, drink, or your body
What to wear? Look at the flowers, they're made intricately
Look at the birds of the air, what's their industry?

Yet I feed and care for them. Then how much more you
Of the birds and trees, who's of greater value?
Isn't life more important than what you worry about—
The mortgage or the rent—even your credit report?

Can you by being anxious add an inch or one hour?
Do you forget that I am the Source of your power?
Why don't you seek my kingdom first, pursue my
righteousness?
You do that, for I've promised that I will do the rest!

My kingdom, child, is not meat or drink.
I know you need these things, what do you really think?
My kingdom is righteousness, joy, and peace
In my presence you will find that they will only increase.

Cast all your cares on me, oh ye of little faith.
Why do my children suffer under such a heavy weight?
Life is more than interest rates, late fees, and bills past due,
Health circumstances, legal woes, social disruptions too.

These devices I use to test out your faith, it's true;
To see if you believe that I will take care of you.
Just understand, the words that I speak cannot
return to me
Until the purposes for which they're sent have been
fulfilled, you see.

I know you need the things you need: house, food, and
clothes, indeed.
But my pleasure is to give you the kingdom that you need.
So take a break from worry, so much you now possess.
Start expressing gratitude, you'll see that you
are blessed."

Index

A

adversity in life 166
advertisements 49, 162
Almighty 46
Ash, Mary K. 110
assessment 119

B

Bible 18, 53, 57, 78, 99, 102, 114
billionaires 165

C

Cain and Abel's offerings 129
cheerfulness 130, 139
children of Israel 165
choice between God and wealth 86
Christian walk 74
commandments 63, 69
commitment 25, 119
compensation 41, 42, 172
contentment 49
covetousness 37
cream of the crop 133
creative survival 110

D

Dayton, Howard 49, 101
discipline 93
discontentment 49
Durkheim, Emile 86

E

employers 81

F

faithfulness 10, 22, 66, 138
fear
 fear of becoming rich 30
 fear of scarcity 142
 fear of success 46
 fear of the Lord 25, 82, 93
financial objectives 154
forgiveness 42, 55
freedom 30, 55, 142
Fuller, Millard 70
future 33, 61, 62, 94

G

gifts from God 10, 117
God
 allegiance to 81
 as Supreme Authority 138
 expectations 133
 kingdom of 18, 22, 30, 34, 102, 151
 preference on offerings 130
 promise 134
 reverence and obedience to 30
 sovereignty 9, 10, 172
 supremacy of 30
 will of 166

gospel 69
gratitude 43, 50, 51, 62, 99, 102, 138

H

Habitat for Humanity International 70
hardship 141, 166, 172
heavenly treasure 70
humility 10, 42, 102

I

inaction 109
inheritance 102, 162
investments 154
Israelites. *See* children of Israel

J

Jeremiah 82
Jesus 21, 33, 41, 42, 54, 57, 69, 70, 74, 109, 137, 150, 173
Job 9, 30, 171

K

King Tut 71

L

law of giving 142
law of love 69
law of Moses 69
laws of the land 158
laziness 113
legacy 158, 162
Levitical law 134
life 34, 50, 69, 73, 85, 101, 157

M

millionaire 25, 26, 70
Miracle Services Inc. 110
money 53
  as a supreme power 30
  love of 54
  negative ideologies 21
  pursuit of 26
  selfish desires for 53, 54
money management 162
  skills 161
  strategies 153
multimillionaire 25, 70
Murray, Andrew 106

N

negative emotions 118
nest egg 70, 154
New York Times 165

P

parable 33, 77, 161, 162
Paul, Saint (the apostle) 49, 62, 142, 169
personal disasters 9
poverty 10, 17, 22, 25, 74, 113, 115, 122
prayer 57, 61, 109
proverb 114
Proverbs 26, 81, 93
psalmist 39, 82, 118, 157
pseudo-Christian ideologies 6

R

reality 78
retirement funds 154
rich people
  bad traits 18
  contributions 18
  perceptions 21
routine 114

S

savings plan 155
scarcity 34, 141
Solomon 5, 30, 73, 82
  God's promise to 21, 22
  teachings of 86
Spirit 7, 46
spiritual character 86
spiritual maturity 172

T

Tada, Joni Eareckson 172
thanksgiving 169
tithe 134, 142, 146
tithing 146, 149

U

unworthiness 42

W

Wall Street 86
wealth 10, 17, 27, 55, 70, 74, 78, 85, 101, 114, 115
wealth-producing abilities 18
White, Dorothy 110
will 158
willingness 26, 141

wisdom 22, 26, 86, 87, 94, 102
Word of God 38, 77, 85, 93, 142. *See* also Bible
  about poverty 17
  principles regarding money 94
  replacing false beliefs through 47
workers 81
worry 62, 78
worthiness 58

Your Money Counts
    49, 101

Notes

1. Ecclesiastes 1:14
2. Matthew 19:24
3. Romans 14:5 (KJV)
4. Job 1:3
5. Job 1:21
6. Psalm 62:10
7. Proverbs 28:6
8. Matthew 25:18
9. Matthew 25:21
10. Ref. Luke 6:20 and 24
11. Deuteronomy 5:6–9a (NASB)
12. Luke 12:20
13. Matthew 6: 25
14. Ref. Genesis 4:8
15. Philippians 4:7
16. Psalm 65:9b and 11
17. Matthew 10:31; Luke 12:7
18. Psalm 139:24
19. 2 Corinthians 2:9
20. Matthew 6:7
21. Mark 9:22b–23
22. Matthew 5:45 (NASB)
23. *Webster's New Universal Unabridged Dictionary*, New York, Barnes & Noble, 1996

24 John 15:5
25 Philippians 4:8
26 Isaiah 43:7
27 1 Thessalonians 5:18 (NLT)
28 Ref. Ecclesiastes 2:11 (NLT)
29 See Isaiah 55:11
30 Ref. Matthew 9:29; Matthew 19:26
31 *The American Heritage Dictionary*
32 Ref. Malachi 3:5; Isaiah 10:1–4
33 Ref. Psalm 37:13
34 Ref. Proverbs 1:8–18
35 http://www.usatoday.com/money/industries/manufacturing/2005–06-17-tyco-timeline_x.htm.
36 2 Chronicles 16:9
37 http://durkheim.itgo.com/suicide.html.
38 Psalm 24:1, 1 Timothy 6:17
39 New International Version Copyright © 1973, 1978, 1984 by International Bible Society Ref. Proverbs 1:7
40 The American Heritage College Dictionary: Third Edition, Houghton Mifflin Company. 1993
41 Proverbs 1:7
42 Proverbs 11:15, Proverbs 22:26
43 James 4:17 (AMP)
44 Proverbs 11:15, 17:18 (NLT)
45 Psalm 25:3
46 Ref. Matthew 25
47 Ref. Matthew 25:28–29
48 Howard Dayton, *Your Money Counts,* Gainesville: Crown Financial Ministries, 1996
49 George Arthur Buttrick, *The Interpreter's Dictionary of the Bible,* Vol. 2., Abingdon Press: New York, 1962

50 Andrew Murray, *Waiting On God,* Great Britain: Lakeland, 1968
51 1 John 3:21–22
52 Joshua 7:10; Exodus 14:15
53 Proverbs 6:10–11
54 Genesis 1:28
55 *The Star-Ledger*, Section 10, November 11, 2007, p. 1.
56 Luke 6:38
57 2 Corinthians 9:7 (NLT)
58 Mark 12:42
59 Luke 6:38
60 2 Corinthians 9:10
61 2 Corinthians 9:10
62 Amos 5:22
63 Matthew 5:23–24
64 Encarta Dictionary: English (North America)
65 Johnson Oatman, Jr., 1856–1922; and Edwin O. Excell, 1851–1921
66 Proverbs 13:22
67 Luke 16:10; 19:17
68 Romans 12:12; Hebrews 12:7, 10; James 1:2–4
69 James 1:4 (NASB)
70 Philippians 4:6
71 John 9:3

www.ingramcontent.com/pod-product-compliance
Lightning Source LLC
LaVergne TN
LVHW050639100826
845148LV00011B/1915

* 9 7 8 0 6 1 5 3 4 4 8 7 4 *